Selling From The Inside Out

Success comes from selling yourself from within before selling yourself from the outside

First edition published by WOW Book Publishing™ and

Vishal Morjaria at WowBookPublishing.com

www.MasterYourWow.com

Copyright ©

ISBN: 9798391781066

All rights reserved. No portion of this book may be reproduced mechanically, electronically, or by any other means, including photocopying, without permission of the publisher or author except in the case of brief quotations embodied in critical articles and reviews. It is illegal to copy this book, post it to a website, or distribute it by any other means without permission from the publisher or author.

Warning — Disclaimer

The purpose of this book is to educate and entertain. The author and/or publisher do not guarantee that everyone following these techniques, suggestions, tips, ideas, or strategies will become successful. The author and/or publisher shall have neither liability nor responsibility to anyone with respect to any loss or damage caused, or alleged to be caused, directly or indirectly by the information contained in this book.

Testimonial 1

Even though I have been a business owner for a number of years, I never really liked selling. I found it boring and sometimes cringey.

However, after reading Navin's book and taking the selling skills and attitude audit, I realised that I didn't have a loving or expansive relationship with sales. The book highlighted to me that in order to fulfil my life's mission, I needed to develop a better relationship with sales.

This book is extremely clear and gives practical steps on how to improve sales from both a mindset and skillset perspective. I am feeling excited about putting into practice Navin's wisdom to reach more people and make an even bigger difference in this world.

Gosia Gorna
International speaker, author and creator of ' The Expansion Game'.

Testimonial 2

This is not like any other sales book that you will ever read! It's brilliantly written, beautifully simple, super easy to understand and blends the worlds of mindset, inner game, selling and performance so that you walk away with not just one skill but everything you need to win. Whether you're a salesperson, an entrepreneur, someone who wants to improve your communication skills, or you want to sell without selling your soul, this book is for you!

Sammy Blindell
The Brand Builder – CEO – How To Build A Brand

Testimonial 3

I have been working with Navin for a few months now on a 121 basis to help me develop myself around sales and to allow me to reach the next stage in my business growth. I would highly recommend investing in Navin if you want to grow your business and develop yourself. He is great at what he does, and what makes him special is his focus on both mindset and skillset when it comes to sales. I am seeing first-hand how important it is to focus on both of these areas, and in the time we have worked together I am seeing myself becoming more confident, and I'm sure that this progress will only continue in the months to come.

Kat Derbyshire
CEO -Black Kat HR

Testimonial 4

I joined Navin's sales workshop as I wanted to develop my sales skills set so that I am better equipped to deal with selling during the economic downturn. I thought it would serve as a useful reminder of best practices, as I have been in sales for 20 years. I found that the workshop far exceeded my expectations. It covered a lot of content that I had never come across previously in a sales workshop. Navin helped me see things from a different perspective when it came to sales and rethink some of my approaches. The workshop gave me valuable new tools that I will implement, and as a result, I am confident it will help me grow my sales during this tough period.

I would thoroughly recommend attending if you are a business owner, sales leader or salesperson.

David Prior
Managing Director – Rentology

Foreword

In today's fast-paced world, success and building a positive brand in the minds of those you want to influence is not just about hard work and talent. It's also about having the right mindset, inner game, and authentic influencing skills. I look back to the year 2002 in the early days of my first business and cringe when I think about all the things I did badly in sales meetings and conversations with people that you'll learn not to do in this book! It took me 18 years in business, nine companies built, and more than six figures invested in sales training and sales coaches before I met Navin and learned that knowing how to sell is just one part of winning clients, projects and prospects. No amount of skills in sales will help you if you don't also master your mindset, inner game and performance. He is spot on.

That's what I love about Navin and what he has created here for you in this book. Literally, right now, you hold in your hands a valuable treasure chest that I wish I'd had when I was where you are right now. It doesn't need to take you the 18 years it took me to master what you are about to learn. But reading this book is just one half of it. Implementing it, testing the strategies in it and applying yourself to the teachings in it is up to you. It's easy to read a book and dabble a little bit in what you learn. But I want you to see this as more than just a book. What you hold in your hands is a beautiful blend of practical and implementable mindset, inner game, selling, and performance strategies to help you become a master of influence in every conversation you have from now on. This is not just a sales book. It's a book that will help you to achieve all your goals - not just sales goals. Whether it's getting a seat upgrade on your next flight, receiving bonuses you didn't ask for, getting free desserts with your next meal, drinks on the house, being able to communicate with your partner in a more supportive way, or winning that next big promotion. The world will be your oyster when you put Navin's teachings into practice!

What I love most about this book is that Navin has drawn on his many years of experience in sales, coaching, and personal development to create this practical and actionable guide that will help you to develop the mindset and skills you need to succeed. He has distilled the best practices from the worlds of sales, psychology, mindset, and performance to create a step-by-step guide for you that will help you to become a master of influence in everything you do. That's why he's my sales mentor, and that's why I recommend him to all of my mastermind members around the world. If you want to:

- Develop a winning mindset that will help you to achieve your goals
- Master the inner game of selling and influence
- Build rapport and connect with people on a deeper, more meaningful level
- Overcome objections and close more sales without selling your soul
- Use the power of language to influence and persuade in a supportive and authentic way

- Develop your inner game to overcome limiting beliefs and boost your confidence

Then you are going to love this book! So, settle in, buckle up and enjoy the ride because your first best decision was to buy this book. Your next best decision will be to take action on it.

With love and blessings, **Sammy Blindell, The Brand Builder, Sammy is a multi-award-winning international speaker, nine times best-selling author, CEO of How To Build A Brand Global, and Founder of One Drop Movement.**

Dedication

I dedicate this book to my late mother, Tripta Jaitly, for bringing me into this world and for giving me all she could in the 16 years I was fortunate enough to spend with her. I know that she would be very happy seeing this book if she was alive today. I am sure she is sitting in Heaven, smiling down in approval.

I also dedicate this book to all of the people who will read it. I hope that it gives you a good understanding of my philosophies and that it helps you on your journey to being the best you!

Table of Contents

Introduction My story 1

Chapter 1 It's all about relationships 5

Your relationship with yourself 5

Your relationship with sales 10

Getting to know your relationship with your product or service 12

Chapter 2 Clarity kills confusion 16

Clarity of purpose 16

Identity 21

Skills 23

Goal Setting – The importance of it 26

Chapter 3 The power of belief 30

Chapter 4 Changing your belief patterns 45

Chapter 5 Don't be afraid 58

Chapter 6 Get laser focused 70

Chapter 7 Develop a winning attitude 76

Chapter 8 The voices within 81

Chapter 9 Bring on the joy. 89

The inner game is summarised. 92

Chapter 10 It's all in the questions 95

Follow up questions............................... 97

Level 1, 2 and 3 questions 98

Chapter 11 104

Remember to listen 104

Chapter 12 Tell me a story 108

Chapter 13 One size doesn't fit all...................... 118

Towards and away from Meta programme 122

Detail and Global Meta Program 123

Sameness and Difference Meta Program- 124

Chapter 14 Influence me. 126

Trust 130

Chapter 15 Always be closing 135

Final thoughts.. 138

Acknowledgements 141

About the Author.. 143

Introduction

My story

I stood at the reception desk of my client's waiting room. They were posh, swanky central London offices. It was a big meeting... make or break for me. I was fairly new both to the world of sales and the company I worked for and hadn't yet sold a thing. I was trying to put on a brave face. I would have appeared confident to the receptionist, who was engaging in chit-chat with me, as I was making small talk with her, laughing and joking. Inside, a very different conversation was going on in my head. Navin, what if you mess this meeting up? You're already behind on your sales quota. Your boss might start losing faith in you. Maybe you're not cut out for a career in sales. After all, you only went into sales because everyone else said you would be a natural. Maybe it's better if you get sacked. At least you'd be put out of your misery. This currently feels like daily torture.

At that point, I zoned back into the conversation and forced myself to laugh at the receptionist's joke. Before I knew it, I was greeted by a man in a grey suit.

It was my client. He was so much taller than I'd imagined him to be. He exuded confidence and seemed very serious. A few minutes later, I was sitting opposite him, and the meeting was underway. I asked a couple of questions, and my client did most of the talking for the first few minutes, which was a relief, but then he asked me a question. I froze. I had forgotten some very important information about the industry. I couldn't believe it; I blurted out an answer that I just made up on the spot, and it was all downhill from that point. The client gave me a look of disdain. He asked me another question related to my answer, but I froze again and had to admit I didn't know. He then asked me if my original answer had been accurate. I dropped my head in shame and admitted I may have got it wrong.

Again, the inner dialogue started. How can you be so stupid? Why did you make up an answer? You should have just said you didn't know. You've lost credibility now. This guy is in a senior position, and he doesn't suffer fools gladly. Somehow, I managed to snap out of my thoughts and zone back into the conversation, but the client spoke less and less; he looked impatient and bored at the same time. I just kept ploughing on with my verbal diarrhoea then, suddenly, I remembered the sales training about how to keep a client engaged. Just keep asking him open questions. I had asked my third consecutive open question when my client held up his hand.

"Stop! I think I've heard enough," he said. "These questions are irrelevant and, frankly speaking, a waste of my time. There's no point continuing this conversation. We won't be buying."

My heart sank. This meeting was worse than I had imagined. It was a total disaster. What went wrong? I followed the sales training, asked the client open questions about his business, sat with confident body language, and listened more than I spoke. I went home that night confused, upset and angry with myself. I felt like sending an email to my boss to resign. Many years have passed since that meeting, and now I can look back at it and laugh. I can honestly say it was one of the best things that happened to me. After that meeting, I had a serious look at what I was doing wrong. I realised the reason I wasn't selling was not that I didn't have the intelligence, the talent, the desire or the training. It was because of the negative inner dialogue that was playing in my head. The dialogue, which I now call the inner game.

A rock-solid inner game is a basic requirement for high performance. This is especially true when it comes to situations where you are required to sell, and it applies whether that be as an entrepreneur selling your service to society, a salesperson selling your product or service to a client, or a public speaker selling your vision to the world. The inner game is like the engine of a car. You can have the best body and wheels (outer game), but if the engine doesn't work, the car will go nowhere. In my experience, elite performers have this sussed.

When it comes to the world of sales, it's so important that you are well-rounded. That means having a rock-solid inner game but also a fantastic outer game. When I refer to the outer game, I mean sales skills such as questioning, listening, communicating, negotiating and strategy etc. Most companies and individuals spend a disproportionate amount of time and money on developing their outer game. This is despite the fact that research has shown that 80% of sales success (I would argue all performance-related success) comes from mindset and emotional mastery. Whilst it's important to develop both your inner game and outer game when it comes to sales, it's more important to develop your inner game. Companies and individuals are often left frustrated and disappointed with their results and often wonder why their investment in coaching or training isn't working.

I have written this book to share my philosophy and explain some of the ways in which you can develop both. I have concentrated on developing sales as a mindset and emotional mastery as I believe that to be more important. I wanted to keep it short so that someone could read it in one or two hours and gain an overview of my philosophy. I could have written so much more, but we live in such a busy world I decided to keep it short so that it's a quick and easy read.

Chapter 1

It's all about relationships

Your relationship with yourself

Everything important in life from a rewarding job to a sense of fulfilment and happiness in your home life can be traced to the quality of your relationships. This includes your boss, your life partner, your parents, your grandparents and your children.

However, the single most important relationship you have is with yourself. How you think of yourself and your sense of identity is of vital importance. This is especially true when it comes to sales, as that image of self is what you project to the world. The more you believe in your abilities, the more confidence and reassurance you will project to potential clients. Therefore, to become truly successful at sales, you must first and foremost have a positive relationship with yourself. Many people don't truly understand the positive and negative attitudes they have towards themselves. I know that this process might seem daunting, so let's take it one step at a time. The first step towards transforming your sales results is to understand your personal relationship and to work on improving the parts that are not so positive.

- Getting to know yourself

Without becoming too philosophical, a great question to ask yourself is – *Who am I?*

Though this might sound very profound and Zen-like, it's an important question. Just ask it of yourself and write down whatever comes up. This will probably cover your views on your personality but might also include your ancestral origins, your home town or your relationships. There's no right or wrong answer. Go ahead – ask it now, and don't think too hard before responding.

The next question to ask is – *What do I think about myself?* To simplify, I have broken this down into the following two points:

- Do I like myself: do I embrace all my features, both positive and negative?
- Do I provide value to the world?

You might initially assume that your answers to these questions will be positive. However, what I have found by doing this exercise with clients, is that they often don't like or embrace every part of themselves. Once you know what you like and dislike about yourself, then, you will become more self-aware. As Buddha said: he who is self-aware has the ultimate power.

If you find these questions difficult, another tip is to break them down by writing a list of what you like and dislike about yourself. I can't overestimate the importance of understanding what we *dislike* about ourselves at a subconscious level. This is often what we avoid and hide from in our daily life. However, whatever we repress comes back ten times harder. For example, let's say you believe that you're too emotional as a person. You, therefore, spend your life suppressing your emotions. Every once in a while, those curbed emotions come flooding out – and rarely in a positive way. This only reinforces your belief that you are too emotional.

- Improving your relationship with yourself

So, now you are aware of the relationship that you have with yourself: all the things you like and dislike, including all your flaws and your insecurities. This is an overwhelmingly positive situation, as you are now in a position to make changes and improve your relationship. So, how do you do this?

- Acceptance

First of all, take a particular flaw or insecurity, and learn to accept it. If this sounds impossible, don't panic. Don't think of it as a problem or disease that is plaguing your life. Just think of it as a part of you – something that shapes your character. The key is to be very neutral in your evaluation of it. Don't exaggerate it, but simply recognise it as something to improve. Once you have a general level of acceptance, you are more likely to tackle it in a positive and balanced way. For instance, say you are aware that you have a short fuse and that you frequently snap at people with little or no justification. Just becoming aware of this flaw is already a positive: you will lose your temper less often –and be inclined to apologise more quickly – because you have accepted this negative as a part of you.

- Adjustment

Once you have accepted it, it's time to move to the next level. Think about your perceived flaw and imagine if it was the opposite and, therefore a strength. Think about how it would feel, what you would think and how you would act. Write this down, so you can envisage it. Imagine yourself and visualise it, as if it were already a strength. Once you have a clear image and understanding of what it would feel and look like for this flaw to transform into a strength, you can take action every day to improve on it. Then, on an everyday basis, you can work on gaining the skills, knowledge and character traits to change the way you think about this perceived flaw.

For example, I used to be very impatient as a person. I knew it was a problem, and it cost me dearly many times. I hated this part of myself and would often beat myself up about it. However, I eventually learned to accept it and realised that my impatience also had advantages, as it made me a man of action and someone who would get things done. By just accepting it, I was in a better mental state to tackle it. I then wrote down, imagined and thought about what it would look and feel like if I was more patient. I thought about how it would benefit my life. I got a really good understanding of this and became excited about improving this part of my personality. Then I took action. I started by introducing meditation and mindfulness into my life so that I could live more in the present. I became more empathetic and compassionate with myself, as well as with other people. This helped me to stop pushing (impatience) and to let situations evolve as they were supposed to.

Finally, I understood that some of my impatience came from a place of insecurity or from a place of fear. I needed to obtain answers or results quickly so that I could feel secure that things would work out well. So, I made the conscious decision to trust myself, others and situations more. This resulted in me naturally becoming more patient, as I didn't feel the need to force a result. This example is one of many ways in which I improved on my perceived flaws. Once I had a better relationship with them, I developed a better relationship with myself. And once I had improved my relationship with myself, I found that everything started to fall into place with less effort on my part.

Once again: the most important relationship you will have in life is the one you have with yourself.

Your relationship with sales

To have success with any activity, you need to have a good, healthy relationship with it. This is especially the case when it comes to something as challenging as sales. Often the main reason why people have a problem achieving a good level of sales is that they have an unhealthy relationship with the noble art. So the first step is to understand your relationship with the field.

- Getting to know your relationship with sales

A great way to start is to close your eyes and see what comes up when you picture a salesperson. For some of my clients, the images that arose were of an oily guy in a cheap suit, who was just interested in making money and did not care about the customer. This exercise can be further illuminated by writing down what comes to you when you think of salespeople. If your images, thoughts and written words are in any way negative, this can give you a good indication of how you will approach sales and the likely results you will obtain.

- Improving your relationship with sales

So, what can you do if these images are negative? A technique called 'image distorting' is very helpful. This is where you close your eyes and picture the negative image that you originally generated, and then, like changing a movie reel, you replace it with a more positive image. For example, if your image is of a pushy, oily, snake-like salesperson in a cheap suit, then replace it with one of a person who is honest, helpful to others and who improves the lives of happy customers. The key is to make both images vivid and then switch them over very quickly – almost as if you're watching a movie reel or a slide show. Repeat this exercise several times a day. The key is to try to put some emotion behind it and to keep a positive image in your mind between exercises.

The next step is to write down all the positive things you associate with sales and salespeople. Write an exhaustive list and look at that list several times a day.

The final step is to write down what your negative perception of sales and salespeople is costing you. How is it affecting your ability to sell, and what implication is that having on your life? Recognising the negative connotations will spur you to make a conscious effort to change your negative thoughts. It will ensure that you follow the first two steps on a daily basis. Note that this isn't a quick fix, and it may well take a few weeks or even months to see the full effects. However, over time, your thoughts and views will change, and you will enjoy a more positive relationship with sales and salespeople. Once this happens, you will approach sales in a more loving, confident, proactive and positive way. This will ultimately result in you making more sales.

Getting to know your relationship with your product or service

The other key relationship that needs to be positive and healthy is the one you have with your product or service. Many business owners and salespeople come to me believing that they have a good relationship with this, but when we scratch the surface together, they come to realise that there are many insecurities lurking there. So, the first step is to understand that relationship.

Again, a great starting point is to close your eyes and picture the product or service, then write down everything that you thought or saw while your eyes were closed. Be honest with yourself.

Next, write down all the things you like and dislike about your product or service.

- Improving your relationship with your product or service

Once you have an understanding of all your negative thoughts and insecurities towards your product or service, you can start working on them.

As with all relationships, you want to make it as positive as possible. Look through your negative thoughts and insecurities, and challenge each one. Imagine that you are in a court of law, and you are defending yourself against your negative perceptions. Make a case against your negative thinking.

For example, when I first started my business, I was full of doubts and insecurities about the product (which was me). I had thoughts like:

'I'm not that experienced as a coach...'

'I was a very good salesperson, but was I a great one?'

'Will anyone want to hire me? There are better coaches who have far more knowledge, etc.'

So, I decided to go through this exercise of challenging each thought. As I did this, I found that a lot of my original thoughts were simply not true. Yes, I wasn't that experienced as a coach, but I had my unique perspective on personal change that had served me well for years. In order to be valid, a unique perspective isn't dependent on experience; my lack of experience was therefore irrelevant. Furthermore, I was a fully accredited coach through the coaching certification I had completed two years earlier – whilst many other coaches weren't even certified and had just learnt to coach through a lot of trial and error.

I am a very good salesperson but am I a great one? When I challenged this thought, I realised that 'greatness' is, to a large extent, based on perception. There is no real way of measuring greatness. Furthermore, a great salesperson doesn't necessarily translate into a great coach/teacher. And then I remembered my sales successes: how I had sold millions of pounds worth of products, how I had sold in multiple industry verticals, and the sales awards and accolades I had received. Most of all, though, I remembered how I had transformed myself from a struggling salesperson to a high achieving one and all the lessons I had learnt along the way. The knowledge I had gained was invaluable and would be useful to help others transform their sales performance. Once I knew this, I understood that my overall experience would make me an excellent coach. I realised that, though there might be more well-known coaches out there, they didn't share my journey and my insights By interrogating my thoughts, I knew that I didn't need to doubt anymore and that I could go forward and enjoy my business venture.

The next step towards believing in your product or service is to get a better understanding of how it can help your customers. One of the quickest ways of doing this is to immerse yourself in positive testimonials that you have received. Don't dismiss them; read and hold on to every word. As humans, we tend to dismiss compliments and hold on tightly to criticisms. A testimonial is a powerful compliment from your clients and should be highly appreciated and respected. Further to written testimonials, speak to your clients. Find out, in detail, how you have helped them and how their businesses and personal life have improved as a result. When you immerse yourself in these conversations and testimonials, you will find that your appreciation for and faith in your product or service will increase greatly.

Once you are aware of the relationship that you have with yourself, with sales and with your product or service – in particular, once you recognise the negative aspects of these relationships – you will be able to address them. Then you will find yourself in a more empowered position to sell effectively. You will be able to help more people, make more money and live a better quality of life.

Chapter 2

Clarity kills confusion

Clarity of purpose

Without clarity, we can't move forward. We will have no conviction in anything we do. We are in a confused state. In this state, we are hesitant and fearful and, over time, find our motivation and drive dwindling. That's why a very important step on the road to sales success (and any success, for that matter) is to achieve absolute clarity regarding what we want and why we want it.

The number one way to gain clarity about what you want in business and life is to become as self-aware as possible. When you are aware of yourself, what you want, whom you want to be and why, then you can move forward with great clarity.

- The importance of your *why*

Nothing great can be achieved without understanding why you want or even need to do it. Humans are most likely to take action when something inside is moved in them – something on an emotional and/or intellectual level. This movement inside is usually linked to their Why. All the great philosophers talk about it; all the great companies have it in their DNA. You will never reach your full potential unless you truly understand that inner calling or your Why. When I have asked this question of my clients, they have generally cited several reasons. However, I have found that there is usually one underlying reason that drives everything else. So, in order to become super successful at sales, it's vital to uncover your reason.

- How do you identify it?

In order to understand your Why, you need to understand yourself better and how you tick. There are several ways to do this. Below are a few of them:

Values – Knowing your values and their order of priority is an important step. We navigate the world through our values. We often intuitively follow them but don't always consciously acknowledge them. When you identify them, this will lead to a better understanding of what's important to you. Furthermore, they can even give you a guide to how you prefer to sell. The first step to knowing your values is to ask yourself the following set of questions:

1. When am I most inspired?
2. What makes me angry?
3. Who are my favourite types of people?
4. Which famous person inspires me and why?
5. What do I enjoy doing?

6. When do I feel most at peace?
7. Which achievement do I feel most proud of?
8. If time and money were not limited, what would I do?
9. What do I never compromise on?
10. What am I most ashamed of in my life?

Answering these questions will give you a good sense of your core values and why they are important to you. Once you are aware of your values on a conscious level, you will be in a much better position to navigate any challenges that come your way. You will start to sell in a way that's aligned with your values; in other words, you will sell more authentically. The more authentic you are when selling, the more likely you are to make sales. You may never have thought about the link between your values and sales before. Many people don't appreciate the strong link between acting in line with their values and effective selling.

As a simple example: if a core value of yours was honesty, and you were selling a product that you didn't believe was beneficial to your customer, you would be in conflict with your value. It wouldn't matter how well trained you were, nor how skilled you were at selling – eventually, the lack of honesty would eat away at you. You would find ways to self-sabotage the sales you were making. Or you would eventually quit.

So knowing your values intimately will help you to know yourself and what you want. This is very powerful when it comes to sales. Clarity breeds conviction, and conviction breeds results.

Another very powerful tool that can be used to understand yourself (including your values) is DILTS logical levels. The famous coach Robert Dilts created a useful model to understand ourselves better and how we can achieve change. The six logical levels are:

- mission/purpose
- identity
- values /belief
- capability
- behaviour
- environment

The diagram below is a good visual representation. The higher levels are more complex and need more thought. However, I have found from personal experience that when we work on them, the other levels look after themselves.

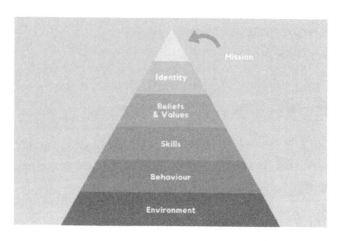

Source - Happy Rubin

Mission/purpose – This is related to your Why. This is your deeper sense of why you do what you do and, at a deeper level, why you are even here (outside the regular surviving and reproducing of the species). Your mission/purpose is usually something that has constantly come up in your thoughts throughout your life. It's something that should evoke or create an inner emotion. Something that drives your inner spirit. It does not have to be that grand a mission, but it should be something that brings out an inner desire that's more than just logical thinking.

Your mission/purpose usually takes a long time to figure out and is often the most difficult part of DILTS logical levels. It can evolve throughout your life. Let's refer back to my story earlier when I was a struggling salesperson. In those days, if you had asked me what my mission was, I wouldn't have known. If you had pushed me for an answer, I would have said something along the lines of 'making sure

I do well enough to keep my job'. As time went on and I progressed as a person, my mission evolved into 'being the best salesperson in the company', and now it has evolved further. Now my ultimate mission is to 'empower millions of people globally so that they achieve their maximum potential'.

Having a strong sense of mission/ purpose (however grand it is) can help you in all other areas of the DILTS logical levels. For example, as my mission is to empower millions of others, it means that I need to create a powerful identity for myself and live fully to my values etc. If I don't do that, then I am unlikely to fulfil my mission.

Identity

Figuring out your identity is an important step. However, it is even more important to figure out your ideal personal identity. This is important because when you do this, you see the gap between the two, and you can work out what you need to do to bridge that gap. Understanding your identity (or ideal identity) is powerful because it gives you a sense of how you need to act on a daily basis. For example, years ago, when I was a struggling salesperson, I would have identified myself as just a salesperson working for XYZ company. As a result, I would have acted in a way that was congruent with being a salesperson. When I interacted with CEO's etc I would have subconsciously acted in an inferior manner as I would have thought of myself as JUST A SALESPERSON.

However, as I developed myself and progressed as a person, I began to see myself as the CEO of my own business within a sales function of the company I worked for. As I internally identified myself as a CEO working for my company, this made a difference in the way I acted around other C-level execs. I started to behave, talk and act in a way that was on their level. As a result, they respected me more and took me more seriously. Now, I am the CEO of my own business, and I am regularly advising and coaching C-level executives. I now identify myself as a CEO and a visionary. I have made a further shift internally and very much behave in a way that is congruent with my internal identity. Creating a self-identity and acting in congruence with that is a powerful step to achieving greater success.

Beliefs and values – This has been and will be covered in this book in more detail. What you believe about yourself, the world, and others and the values you hold dearest are important to know. These form a key part of the way you think and act. When I was a struggling salesperson I believed that I was an average salesperson (at best), and I didn't rate myself that highly. I valued safety, and for me, it was important to keep hold of my job at any cost. I was focused on avoiding getting the sack because I believed I was not that good. When I developed myself and became more successful, I changed my beliefs and values. I then believed that I was a very good salesperson and I started to rate myself. My values changed and became more positive. I now valued success, reward (commission) and recognition (sales awards and boat trips). My focus went from surviving to thriving within my role. Now my values and beliefs have evolved even further. I believe that I am a world-class salesperson, coach and trainer. I value personal mastery and becoming the best version of myself.

Skills

These are the capabilities and competencies that you have developed. These are what you are (and what you think you are) good at. Identifying and understanding our skills is important, as these can make us feel and act confidently. When I was a struggling salesperson I didn't have a solid base of sales skills. More importantly, I didn't feel like I had a solid base of sales skills. As a result, I wouldn't feel confident in closing deals. As I saw fewer results, I would invest less time and effort in developing my skills because I didn't think it would be worth it. However, over time (and the more successful I became), the more skills I gained. As I got more wins under my belt, it encouraged me to invest even more time and effort into developing my skills. I now invest a significant amount of time, effort and money in keeping myself highly skilled.

Carrying out a skills audit of yourself is a very useful exercise. As a salesperson or leader, it's a good idea to write down an exhaustive list of the skills and capabilities that you have. You will often be surprised by how many there are. Knowing how many skills you possess can further boost your confidence. It can also serve as a reminder of the skills that you need to develop in order to become the person you want to be and to achieve your mission.

Behaviour – This relates to how you typically show up and how you want to show up. Your behaviour is the actions you take and how you interact with those around you. Your behaviours are often driven by the higher DILTS levels (Mission, Identity etc.). For example, early in my career, the behaviours I exhibited were indecisive, unassured, defensive, pessimistic and unconfident. These behaviours were mainly negative, and as a result, I wouldn't have as powerful interactions with my clients. When I developed my inner game, I started to exhibit different behaviours. My behaviour was more confident, direct, optimistic and brave. This resulted in me having much better and more powerful interactions with clients. One of the most effective ways to change your behaviours is to tap into the higher DILTS levels. For example, because my current mission is to empower millions globally so they reach their maximum potential, that means I make sure that I exhibit the behaviours that will help me reach my mission. I show up every day optimistic, focused, confident and driven.

Taking the time out to evaluate how you behave and how you want to behave ideally can be a powerful exercise.

Environment – This is the one part of the DILTS model that is more externally than internally focused. It can make a big difference in our levels of success. Our environment is the external world around us. It's where we work, live, socialise etc. It can play an important role in shaping who we are. Many people who grow up in tough, crime-ridden environments are more likely to become criminals themselves. When people are exposed to pleasant environments, they tend to become more pleasant.

Note, however, there can be a difference between what our environment is and what we perceive it to be. For example, when I was struggling in sales, I thought that the corporate environment was a tough, cut-throat and dangerous place. However, when I became a successful salesperson, I thought that the same environment was fun, exciting and a great playground of opportunity.

Taking an assessment of your environment (perceived or real) is important. By knowing this, you are able to make a judgement on whether the environment is right for you and your aspirations.

Once you have identified your Why (with the help of some of the tools above) and achieved clarity over what you want, it's important to move on to the next step. Know your goals and what you are looking to achieve.

Goal Setting – The importance of it

Setting goals is a fundamental part of success. It gives you long-term vision and short-term motivation. It helps you to focus and to organise your time and resources so that you can make the most of your life. This is so important when it comes to sales. When you have clear and measurable sales goals, then you will be propelled to take action to make them happen. Goals give you direction and focus. In sales, you need clarity and focus. It might sound obvious, but you will be surprised how few people have clear and measurable sales goals. Even if they do have them, they haven't thought them through. They have just come up with arbitrary numbers. A salesperson or entrepreneur without clear goals is like an explorer without a compass; you will eventually go round and round in circles. You can be as motivated as you want, but without knowing what you're aiming for, you will eventually become stuck. As a result, your motivation will wane, and you will eventually give up.

In order to make a goal effective, it helps if it is **SMART**

- Specific – Make the goal as specific as possible. Simple to understand and significant to business success. For example – Increasing turnover
- Measurable – The use of a milestone or marker to measure success

- Achievable – Realistically achievable by all stakeholders
- Relevant – Plays a key part in the wider business strategy
- Time-bound – Must be measured within a specific time frame

SMART sales goal example – I will increase month-on-month turnover by £15000 for the next 12 months. This will be achieved by onboarding two new clients a month with an average customer value of £7500 a month

This goal is clear in what needs to be achieved (increasing turnover), how it will be achieved (onboarding more customers) and when it will be achieved (every month for the next 12 months)

I do have one major problem with SMART goals, though, and that is the Achievable part. I find that when you are evaluating whether something is achievable or not, what you are asking yourself is, 'Can I really do this?' The problems with being overly realistic are twofold: First of all, the human mind tends to play things safe and, therefore, usually downplays what is realistic. The second reason is that we tend to base what is realistic on either what other people around us have achieved or on our past results. The problem with that, is we have to be very careful about whom we compare ourselves to. Often our colleagues or business acquaintances are more or less on the same level as us. That means we are failing to compare ourselves to someone (or a business) who is at a higher level - the level we aspire to. We are already playing things too safe.

When we base our goals on what we have achieved before, then we are already limiting our minds to what's possible. Furthermore, if we are constantly evolving and improving, then we should automatically be setting our sights much higher. I am not suggesting that we create crazy goals that there is virtually no chance of achieving. However, I find that the A (achievable) in SMART often limits people from stretching their minds and pushing their boundaries to a higher goal. I would suggest then when setting a SMART goal, replace Achievable with Ambitious. I believe that if business owners, salespeople and sales leaders did this, they would fast-track their results.

SMART goal setting is a widely known concept. It is successfully used by many salespeople all over the world. What really brings the SMART goal to life, however, is when you bring emotion to it. The emotion is what brings the energy and fuel. The emotion comes from a deeper part of you, usually what's nestling in your subconscious brain. It's your true motivation for achieving that goal. SMART goals are a conscious brain activity. Therefore, the combination of creating SMART goals (using your conscious brain) and linking those to your subconsciously driven reason for wanting to achieve those goals will ensure that you are much more likely to smash through your sales goals.

Training your subconscious mind to set goals -

The subconscious mind is our most powerful tool. It can literally make or break a goal.

We hear so much about the subconscious mind. The subconscious mind takes the information you give it and does its best to make sure that information remains true. For instance, if you tell your subconscious mind, "I'm not realistically going to achieve that goal I've set," it will do its utmost to make sure that piece of information is true unless and until you replace that belief with another. The most effective goals are based on, or linked to, something that's important to you. Furthermore, it's important that we check that, at a subconscious level, we believe we can achieve it. If we don't, then no amount of planning or SMART goal-setting will work.

Our SMART goals give us direction, but our subconscious mind determines if we hit them or not. 90% of our life is run by our subconscious. If we set a goal, but our subconscious mind is not aligned with it, then we will find it much more difficult to achieve.

Once you are crystal clear on what you want and why you want it at both a conscious and subconscious level, you have achieved the important step of clarity.

Chapter 3

The power of belief

For me, this is the most important aspect of success in sales (and for success in life). If you don't believe in yourself or your product or service, then ultimately, you have very little chance of making the sales you want.

Quote – Venus Williams – 'You have to believe in yourself when no one else will – that makes you a winner right there.'

Belief is the energy, the rocket fuel that keeps you going. Our minds are hard-wired to focus on the negative and what can go wrong. Belief is what will help you push through the moments of negativity and self-doubt. Every great athlete, entrepreneur, salesperson and leader has possessed a great amount of self-belief.

How do you develop it? It is one thing to know how important belief is, and another to develop it fully. People with a high level of self-belief have often formed this during their childhood or early adulthood. These people find it a lot easier to believe in themselves and believe in things working out for the best when they are adults. However, there are tools that can be used for those who do not believe in themselves in the same way. Developing a strong level of self-belief is vitally important for business owners, sales leaders and sales professionals.

The belief audit – The first thing to do when developing your self-belief is to take an audit of where you're at. This is a simple process that can be achieved by answering the following five important questions:

On a scale of 1 to 10

1. How much do I believe in myself to hit the goals I set for myself?
2. How much do I believe in good things working out for me?
3. How much do I believe in the product/ service/ company that I'm selling
4. How much do I believe that I am great at what I do (Sales, Leadership etc)?
5. How much do I believe that sales, selling and salespeople are good and needed in this world?

If your number is below 5, it means your level of belief is on the lower side. Scores of 6 -7 indicate average belief levels and scores of 8 and above indicate strong levels of belief. This is a quick health check and a very simple process, but it can serve as a useful tool.

Once you have a better awareness of your belief levels, you can start to work on them and make them stronger. This isn't an easy process and can take some time, but with consistent effort and practice, it can be achieved.

Before we look at some of the methods you can use to develop your belief, let's remind ourselves of the power of belief throughout history; how people have used belief to achieve success.

The four-minute mile – Before 1954, nobody in recorded human history had ever run a mile in under four minutes. Many said that it was physically impossible and was even dangerous to attempt. They said it never had been and never would be achieved. Then on May 6th 1954, 25-year-old Roger Bannister became the first man in history to break it. What people said was impossible had been achieved! When they asked Roger afterwards what was the secret to his success, he listed a variety of factors such as diet and exercise etc. However, he said the single biggest reason was that he believed it was possible. He believed he was capable of doing it. He regularly visualised himself crossing the finishing line in under four minutes. This further increased his belief, and he felt that he had already achieved the milestone before actually doing it in reality. Had Roger not believed it, he either wouldn't have even attempted it or his brain would have stopped pushing his body to achieve it. He even said that at one point, he had felt temporary blindness when running, but he pushed through as he knew he could do it. What's equally remarkable is that just 46 days after he achieved the feat, another person did, and just a year later, three people did so in a single race. Over 200 people broke it in the next 25 years.

So why was it that for thousands of years, nobody could break this barrier, and yet once it was broken, it became a fairly regular occurrence? The answer is simple. It's because they believed it was possible. They had removed the mental barrier that had been holding them back. Roger had a great rival named John Landy. Landy was more talented and renowned than Roger and had narrowly missed out on achieving it in December of 1952, running the race in four minutes and two seconds. After missing out he told the journalists the following "Frankly, I think the four-minute mile is beyond my capabilities. Two seconds might not sound much, but to me it's like trying to run through a brick wall. Someone may achieve the four-minute mile the world is wanting so desperately, but I don't think I can."

Unlike Bannister, Landy didn't believe it was possible to achieve the feat. His repeated failures and that of others cemented his belief that it was impossible. One of the reasons that Roger Bannister believed it was possible was because of the theory of self-efficacy (developed by the psychologist Albert Bandura). According to Bandura (1997), self-efficacy is defined as 'beliefs in one's capabilities to organise and execute the courses of action required to produce given attainments.'

The theory suggests that people with high levels of self-efficacy are more likely to take action towards their goals, persist in the face of adversity and push the barriers of what is deemed possible. So, even though Landy was the better runner technically, he lacked the self-efficacy that Bannister had. Bannister's high levels of self-efficacy helped him to push himself and achieve the seemingly impossible.

This example can be taken into the business, and in particular, the sales world. A salesperson, business owner or sales leader who is pursuing a difficult target and lacks the belief that it will be achieved is always going to underperform, despite how technically proficient they are.

Self-efficacy is built through learning how to reframe failures and obstacles as opportunities for growth. It is also essential to remain committed to the process of achieving something and to avoid not overly attaching yourself to the outcome. At the same time, we should not strive for perfection or beat ourselves up after a mistake.

Another example of the power of belief in history was when Henry Ford instructed his engineers to construct a V8 engine. At the time, his engineers told him that it was physically impossible to construct the engine. However, Henry disagreed and told them to go away and make it. Six months passed, and they still could not do it and told him again that he was asking for the impossible. Another year passed, and the same thing happened. Once again, his engineers told him to give up on this dream and give them something else to work on. He told them that it was possible and not to come back to him until it was made. Eventually, as if by miracle, they finally constructed the famous V8 engine. Henry Ford's unwavering belief (along with the skills of his team) made this happen. If he hadn't believed, he would have given up.

The examples above highlight the power of belief and are very relevant to selling. Sales can be tough and we will face many setbacks and rejections. The most powerful way to overcome them is to have total faith and belief that you will succeed. However, this can't be a false belief where you just tell yourself all will be fine but deep inside think the opposite. In order to increase the belief that we will achieve our sales goals (or any other goal) it's vital that we initially develop the belief and confidence in ourselves. So how do we do this?

Think it's your duty – The first step is to accept that it's your responsibility to develop your level of self-belief and confidence. Once you do this then you will proactively go out of your way to develop them rather than just relying on chance or your mood. When you take responsibility for this then you are likely to create a plan and put things in place that will develop your confidence and belief.

Create a plan- Just like anything else you are trying to build (muscles, stamina, money etc.), a plan makes it much easier to do so. Therefore, you must schedule a time that you will put aside where you will undertake activities that build your belief. Just like you would schedule a time to do back stretches or a morning walk, similarly, you must incorporate confidence and belief-building exercises into your daily/ weekly routine. It's also a good idea to use a coach or trainer to speed up the process.

Create a win list – A very effective way of developing your belief is to create a list of wins you have experienced in your life (these can be both sales and non-sales related). Doing this will remind you of just how successful you already are. This, in turn, will subtly change your self-perception to a more positive and confident one. Think outside of the box when making this list. For example, it could be that you include a time that you overcame difficult odds or that you include an example of something you were failing at but in the end turned around. Examples could be:

- I hated and struggled at making cold calls, but through hard work and persistence, I got myself to an acceptable level
- I turned around my social shyness into becoming a sociable person
- I won a £500,000 contract with Samsung
- I was promoted in my last role to sales manager in a year
- I gained a degree in Dance

It doesn't matter what you put down as long as it happened and it makes you feel happy or proud when you write it down. As long as it meets that criterion then write it down. Over time you might want to break your win list into different sections such as personal wins, sales wins, money wins etc. When putting this list together, it is essential to focus on how it makes you feel. It should make you feel really good about yourself, and it should also remind you of the good things that have happened to you. Getting into this state is very important, as high performance is often a reflection of the states we are in (more about different states later in the book).

Over time you can keep adding to your list, either when you remember something else that was a win in your past or when you experience a brand-new win in your life. You can create future success by looking back at past wins.

This is where looking at client testimonials can be a powerful tool in addition to your win list. This is powerful because it's what other people have positively said about you, your business or your product/service. It can serve as a great reminder of the value that you bring to the world.

One of my clients once asked me what the best way to prepare before a sales meeting was. I asked him what he thought, and he replied by saying all of the obvious things such as: 'Have all the information about the client ready, research about the person you're about to meet, remind yourself of the strengths and weaknesses of his competitors.' Whilst this is all good and should be included, he missed the most important thing. The most important thing that you need to do to prepare for a sales meeting (especially immediately before one), is to get yourself into a state of total belief and confidence. The most effective way of doing this is to revisit previous testimonials and your win list. When you are in a confident and empowered state, you are more likely to make the sale.

Affirmations –These can be a powerful tool when it comes to changing or developing your self-belief. Studies prove that positive affirmations help activate parts of the brain that are associated with self-related processing and reward. The same studies also indicate that positive affirmations can help build or restore self-competence. Positive affirmations are statements or phrases that, when repeated daily, can help challenge negative thoughts and boost self-confidence.

Affirmations also work if you have a repetitive negative thought that causes you to feel bad, but you replace it with an empowering thought. It helps to repeat it to yourself regularly, such as when the negative belief is triggered and at predetermined times of the day. In that way, you practise this new belief, helping it become ingrained into your implicit, automatic memory. Over time this thought becomes habituated, and you believe it. After you have created your affirmations, the next time you catch yourself thinking one of those repetitive negative thoughts, you can remind yourself of the new positive thought you've created to replace it. Because it's something you repeatedly do, using this new thought helps slow the momentum of the negative thought much faster

To understand how positive affirmations work and how you can make the most of them, we have to understand the concept of neuroplasticity, which is the ability to rewire the brain.

The brain is incredibly sophisticated and complex; however, it can get a little mixed up on the difference between reality and imagination. This very loophole serves as the basis of self-affirmation.

When you repeat affirming statements daily, you're helping your brain create a mental image of the goal you're trying to achieve or the version of yourself you are aspiring to become. When this mental image is created, it activates the parts of the brain that would be activated if you were to experience the goal you're trying to achieve in real life. In other words, you're tricking your brain into accepting that the words you are saying about yourself are factually true. This, in turn, will convince it (You) to take action towards your goals. Ultimately, it's the actions that you will take that will help you reach your goals. The affirmations on their own will not. However, they will create the internal belief and confidence needed to take big and bold action.

The 4 Ps for Successful Affirmation Statements are

1. Personal (I, Me statements)

2. Passion (put emotion into it)

3. Present (as if it's already happening, not future)

4. Positive (avoid words like "not" or "don't")

Lastly, you must repeat it REGULARLY.

Potential affirmations you can use when it comes to sales are

- I am a gifted salesperson
- I am passionate about selling
- I have sales flowing into my life
- I have customers who are excited about buying from me
- I love selling

Visualisation – Just like affirmations, visualisations are not magic. However, their effectiveness has been scientifically proven. It is a technique that has been used a lot by athletes over the years and has led to success.

Many people think that visualisation is just fantasy or positive mumbo jumbo, however when you understand how the mind works, then you can begin to comprehend the science associated with it.

Janette Hynes and Zach Turner talk about this in their neuroscience journal Impulse.

They explain a study in which Student-athletes were asked to positively visualise themselves performing physical lifts that they frequently executed in their training regimen (bench press, back squat, clean or deadlift). A directionality analysis demonstrated that, compared to athletes who did not, participants who positively visualised had a significant increase in weight moved during a lift. The positively visualising group demonstrated a 10-15 lb. increase in weight moved, while the control group only demonstrated a 5 lb. increase. This suggested that athletes were more effective when they incorporated positive visualisation into their training.

The power of visualisation is often not well understood. Too often, there is a concept of visualisation being just fantasy or mood-making. When we have a broader understanding of how the mind works and the impact of the mind-body connection, then we can comprehend the amazing science of visualisation. For example, a study of building muscle mass contained two groups. One group participated in actual physical exercise and saw a 30% increase in muscle during the study. The second group visualised performing exercises in their minds only and still showed a 13.5% increase in muscle mass. Not only that, this increase persisted three months after the visualisation training. This is concrete scientific evidence of the power of visualisation.

Visual imagery also fits into the topic of visualisation. It is a well-known fact that the majority of humans are predominantly visual when it comes to the five senses. Therefore, generally speaking, we learn best and are most motivated and inspired to take action through the things we see. That is why companies create visual logos, countries create flags, and football teams have emblems. These are visual representations of these entities and can arouse emotions based on the viewer's internal representation of them. Therefore we can use visual imagery when it comes to shifting our self-belief. One example of this is Vision Boards. These can be very powerful, as the viewer is constantly reminded of the thing that he or she is looking to attain. This will ensure that they are reminding their subconscious brain to take action in order to attain those things. To add to that, they work in a similar way to the mental visualisation technique that Roger Bannister used. By seeing the images on the vision board, you will subconsciously start to believe that they are already part of your life. As a result, you will start to think and act in a way that is more likely to make them your actual reality. For example, if you had included a picture of a Ferrari on your vision board, over time, you would begin to subconsciously believe that you will have one as part of your life. As a result, you are more likely to put in the work needed and gain the skills required in order to make the sales needed to purchase a Ferrari.

This is just one example of how visual imagery can increase the belief needed to become more successful.

Take action – For me, action is central to getting the results needed in sales (and life). Without action, everything is just a fairy tale. Although I do think that people tend to take more action when their levels of self-belief are higher (belief does fuel a lot of action), taking action even when belief levels are on the low side can, in turn, help to grow levels of self-belief. It's a bit like chicken and egg. You may procrastinate and overthink things because you are full of fear and lack the belief needed to take positive action. However, if you are able to get over this and force yourself to take action, you will find that after a while the mere fact you have taken some action will deliver you some results. By getting these results, your levels of belief will increase.

It is better to take action when your belief levels are high, as this is likely to increase the chances of achieving the desired outcome. However, taking action when belief levels are low can often yield results and, in turn, increase our levels of self-belief.

The right tribe –The people you regularly associate with are critically important when it comes to having an optimistic mindset and enhanced levels of belief. If you surround yourself with positive people who also have higher levels of self-belief, then this will rub off on you. Furthermore, when you see that they are achieving success, you will begin to believe that you can do the same as you see that it's possible. That is often why those who join high-performing sports or sales teams increase their personal levels of success. They see others doing well and start to believe it's possible for them to do the same.

Belief is a huge topic and could be explored in a lot more detail. In summary, it is a primary fuel that feeds success. When you believe you can do something or that a successful outcome is possible, then you will start to think, behave and take the actions needed to make it happen. I believe that people should dedicate more time to actively work on their belief muscles. It needs to be trained, just as you would train your shoulders in the gym. Most people, teams and companies rely purely on chance for people to develop beliefs. They think that when someone gets some wins under their belt, then their belief levels will be sorted. Belief needs to be worked on. By using some of the tools I have listed above and doing so consistently, you can raise your levels of belief and achieve successful outcomes.

Chapter 4

Changing your belief patterns

In the last chapter, we looked at developing your self-belief. Now we will look at changing your belief patterns. A lot of our success in sales (and in life in general) comes down to our internal beliefs, thoughts and patterns.

Your belief system is deeply ingrained within you, and it forms your perception of reality. We have filters through which we see and experience the world. We must be aware of our filters and beliefs. This way, we can see if they are negative and in any way stopping us from achieving the results that we desire.

We often build up belief systems to protect ourselves and simplify our lives. However, sometimes, they can do the exact opposite.

For example, let's say that you felt that salespeople are only after making a sale and don't care about your needs. If you work in sales this can be a negative belief with negative consequences for you as, if you believe this to be a fact, it will affect the way you sell. At a subconscious level, you will think that your customers don't trust you and, as a result, your actions will be tentative and potentially negative.

Becoming aware of a belief like that is valuable, as you can then go about changing it to something more positive. So how do you do this?

Step 1: – Identify your beliefs. Write down all your beliefs when it comes to the following:

- Yourself when it comes to business/ sales
- Salespeople and selling
- Your product or service
- The company you work for or business you run

Next, identify which of those beliefs you consider to be negative and which of them you consider to be positive (people are often surprised to discover how many undercover negative beliefs they hold).

Now you will have two lists and a good awareness of your beliefs in the above areas.

Step 2: – Ask yourself where did those beliefs come from? Let's assume that one of your beliefs was as follows:

The company I work for isn't the best in the market. XYZ (competitor) has better products.

This is a negative belief that will affect sales performance. So next, you would ask yourself,

'Where did this belief come from? How and when was it formed?'

For example, you might find that this was formed after hearing a couple of existing customers complaining about your products and praising your competitor.

Most of our core beliefs were formed in childhood. Some research says that up to 80% of our core beliefs were formed in the first 10 years of our life. Our subconscious brain (more on this later) is what's mainly running our life to the age of around six. Therefore, a lot of what we are fed (mentally) as a child becomes a strong part of our beliefs and core personality.

For example, assume we grew up in a household where there was an atmosphere of turbulence and fear, perhaps because of money or illness or violence etc. In that situation, we are likely (although this isn't a guarantee) to become fear-based people at our core. We are likely to be more sensitive to certain things in life that trigger our fears. Some people would call this triggering our inner child. When we are children, we are not able to use logic and reasonable judgement, and our view of the world is based on the feelings we have when we experience something. A lot of the time, these can be irrational fears that aren't true. For example, as a child, we may have seen our parents regularly argue about money. Our child self may have come to the assumption that money is a bad thing. Or it could have gone in the exact opposite direction and generated the thought that money is the route to peace and without it, you can't have peace. Neither of those thoughts are true. Money is not a bad thing and can bring many benefits to a person's life, although it is not the solution to having a peaceful life, and you can have one without money. The beliefs we form about ourselves and the world in childhood become deeply ingrained.

Another example how we form beliefs about ourselves in childhood. We might have been scolded by an adult for expressing an unwanted opinion that challenged them. They might not have even scolded us particularly badly, but for some reason that could have been quite traumatic for our child self (especially if it occurred several times). Our child self might have concluded that expressing your opinion and challenging someone in authority equals bad consequences. As an adult, we become more reasonable in our thought processes, and logic tells us that sometimes expressing certain opinions and challenging people can put us in trouble and other times it won't. However, our deep subconscious thoughts are way more powerful and will remain lurking underneath the surface. So even though we might logically think something, at a deeper level, we may think the exact opposite.

The situation I have described above could play out in our adult lives as a salesperson. For example, if we believe at a subconscious level that expressing an opinion or challenging someone will give us negative consequences, then we will avoid it. As a result, we could be selling to a CEO (person in authority) and avoid expressing a controversial opinion or challenging a particular thought they have expressed. This might end up making us lose out on the sale. A lot of research has been carried out into top-performing sales reps, and that research concludes that those who challenge a customer outperform those who don't. There was a book called 'The Challenger Sale' (written by Brett Adamson and Matt Dixon) that did extensive research into this and found it to be true.

Once the business world found out about the challenger sale concept, they invested a lot of time and money into training people on how to effectively challenge clients, from questioning techniques to how to phrase a sentence when challenging. However, all of this skill-based training will make the minimum difference if the salesperson has a deeply held belief blocking their success.

The example above shows how a negative and irrational belief held subconsciously from childhood can affect the way we behave as adults, how it can affect the way we sell, and, ultimately, our sales results.

Another point to remember about our subconscious brain is that it will believe the more dominant thought that we hold. It will override what we consciously tell ourselves. For example, let's say that, consciously, we are telling ourselves that we want and deserve success. We could even spout a list of reasons why that is if someone asked us. However, if deep down in our subconscious, we hold different beliefs, then our subconscious will believe those thoughts over those we are consciously telling ourselves. If, for some reason, we believe that we don't deserve success, we are not capable of the level of success that we want, or we feel guilty about receiving that level of success, then our subconscious will believe those thoughts more than what we are consciously telling ourselves. As a result, we are more likely to self-sabotage and allow those thoughts to get in the way of achieving our successful outcomes. This will be without even realising we are doing it.

Let's apply this to a sales example. Let's say you really want to smash your sales target every year. You want to become a consistent and high-performing salesperson. You know the reasons why you can achieve that and why you want to achieve it. However, deep down, your subconscious mind doesn't believe you are that person or doesn't believe you deserve that success. Then, without realising, you will probably do things to prevent your success. For example, you might become over-anxious about a deal not closing and, as a result, push the customer too hard, resulting in sabotaging the sale. Or you might do the opposite and not take enough action, not act in a brave manner as you're worried about losing a deal. You might even start getting some consistent results and then start to slack off or change the strategy that was getting you the results in the first place. The bottom line is that because deep down, your subconscious beliefs are in opposition to your conscious ones, you will always revert to them. Ultimately your long-term level of success will match your subconscious beliefs. This is why it's important to understand what they are and to go start rewiring them if they are negative. This can take a lot of work (depending on how negative and how ingrained they are). Through exercises and tools such as affirmations, hypnotherapy, journaling, neuro linguistic programming, coaching and visualisation, it can be achieved.

Our brain – Without getting too technical, the human brain has effectively three parts:

Part 1 is our reptilian brain or basal ganglia (the oldest formed part of the brain). It is part of our brain in charge of our flight, flight and freeze response to life situations. Its primal function is to keep us safe and let us survive (it includes our primitive need to reproduce in order for our species to survive). It is similar to that found in all living creatures whose primary function is to survive and reproduce.

Part 2 is our Limbic brain or paleo mammalian cortex. It is where our Amygdala is seated. Though this is closely linked to our reptilian brain, it is more in charge of controlling our range of emotional behaviours (fear, rage, anxiety etc). It is also thought of in some circles as our subconscious brain. It's where our deep-seated memories, beliefs and emotions are held. It is primarily what a large part of this book is focused on.

Part 3 is our Neocortex brain and where our cerebral cortex is seated. It's often thought of as the newest and most evolved part of our brain.

Now that you know where this belief came from, you can go to step 3

Step 3 – Challenge the belief. – This is where you question how viable the belief is. You could find out how many of your company's clients are delighted with their products and keep buying from them. You could think that the clients you did hear complain about the products were not an accurate representation and were the exception rather than the norm. You may find that many customers complain about your competitors' products. There are many reasons that you can find that can dispel your belief and as a result, start making you doubt it.

Step 4 – Replace it – Now that you have doubt regarding your existing negative belief you can go about replacing it with something more positive. You would have had to go through the previous step in order to effectively implement step 4. For if you still had a doubt, then your mind would not accept the new belief that you were trying to introduce and would have battled against it.

So now think of a new more positive belief you want to replace it with. Make it something that you find credible to make sure your mind is able to accept it. This could be something along the lines of My company has great products which are every bit good as company XYZ.

Step 5 - Now that you have your new belief, the key is to repeat it as often as possible. This can be done in a variety of ways. Here are a couple

- As a mantra/affirmation - This is simply repeating your new belief either out loud or in your head as often as possible
- Talking about your new belief to other people. By discussing it then, it will more likely set comfortably in your mind

Step 5 is an important step as the power of repetition sets in and ensures that over time the new belief stays with you

Before we leave the topic of beliefs, this is a good time to gain a better understanding of where else our beliefs have come from.

We have already discussed how most of them are formed in our childhood. However, they also are formed elsewhere:

Our community - The people we associate with can make a big difference in what we start believing (especially if we associate with them for a prolonged period). This becomes even more apparent if we spend time with a group of people who have a strong set of beliefs. For example, someone could not have many religious beliefs, but if they spent a lot of time with a group of religious people over a long period, they might find that they start to change their beliefs and become more religiously inclined. This is why the influence of culture or community can be so powerful.

So how does this relate to sales, you may ask? Well, let's take a salesperson who is working in an organisation that is very aggressive in its thinking. They hire aggressive salespeople, they sell aggressively, and they do whatever it takes to get the deal in. When this company makes sales, they require the sales people to talk about how they won the deal through their aggressive sales tactics. As a result, the belief that being aggressive is needed to win sales is reinforced. Over time, that salesperson might start to take on the belief of his/ her colleagues, even though he previously didn't believe it. Therefore, it is very important to choose carefully the people you associate with.

The two most powerful factors that shape our beliefs are our upbringing and who we regularly associate with. Below is a list of a few other factors that shape our belief

- The media
- Leaders
- Books
- Music
- Visiting other cultures/ countries

Whilst all of the above can shape our beliefs, our core beliefs are formed in our childhood. Therefore, try the following exercise:

Close your eyes and take several deep breaths. Try to become as relaxed as possible. Then think back to your earliest life memories and incidents that happened to you. See if anything comes up that you think had a major impact on you at the time. Try not to reason with it. For example, you might remember being late for your first day at school and feeling inadequate walking into the classroom with all the other kids looking at you, and the teacher pointing out in annoyance that you were late. You may have felt as if you stood out from the others as a result of being late and wished that you had been on time. You might think that is insignificant and doesn't mean anything and therefore dismiss that memory.

However, I would encourage you to write it down. Keep repeating this process until you can think of four or five early life memories that had a big impact on you at the time they happened. Once you have this list of memories and how they made you feel, then write down what you believed at the time as a result of the incident. So if we take the example above, then you might have felt inadequate for walking into the classroom late and standing out. Therefore you might have taken on the belief at that time that standing out was a bad thing and should be avoided at all costs. Once you have a list of beliefs that you think you may have formed at the time, then the final step is to think about how those beliefs influence the way you sell as an adult. If we take the example above, then perhaps you still shy away from standing out too much because of some of these deeply held beliefs from childhood. This could be having an impact on the way you sell and the results that you get.

Another exercise that you can use to understand your beliefs and recreate them if they don't serve you is to answer the following questions

- What is the belief?
- What am I assuming in order to believe this?
- Is there a deeper belief or fear beneath this?
- When do I first remember having this belief and feeling this way?
- What experience did I have to make me believe this?
- Could I have misinterpreted it? Was there another perspective or other information I may have missed?
- Who do I know that thinks this way or expressed this belief to me?
- What benefits did they receive from believing it or telling me to believe it?

Keep probing and asking yourself until you get to the core of the belief, then summarise the core, underlying belief.

- What would you like to believe instead?
- How does having this new belief make you feel?

56

- Thinking back to the original negative thought and the reason behind it, how have your feelings about it changed?

Chapter 5

Don't be afraid

Fear is something that we will all experience and is a natural part of life. The human brain has evolved so that one of its primary functions is to identify and evaluate danger. Therefore, we are coded with fear built into our programming. One of the most important factors when it comes to our success in sales is how we handle fear.

Fear arises when we feel the threat of harm, whether that is physical, emotional or psychological, real or imagined.

Fear is like fire. Use it well, and it serves you. You can cook and keep warm. Let it get out of control, and it will burn you. Fear causes salespeople to get tired. They become tired due to psychological fatigue. A salesperson will complain about being stressed out and tired, but as soon as they bring in a deal (or have major progress) on a deal, they are re-energised. A salesperson who operates with fear of losing out on a deal or not making quota increases their chances of their reality coming true. This is because they have entertained a thought and vision in their head that vibrates fear. When a salesperson allows their fear to get out of control, allowing it to spark limiting beliefs in their mind, they open themselves up to failure.

Fear is the exact opposite of belief. When you increase your levels of belief, then you increase your chances of success. When you increase your fear, then you increase your chance of failure. I am not suggesting that you act in a fearless manner all the time, or don't look at things that can go wrong. Doing that is practical and can help you to set up processes that help to reduce the chance of failure. However, you don't want your fear to become so out of control that it burns you. Often our fears are in our heads, and the reality of them coming true is small.

Fear also gets in the way of receiving positive thoughts or information. It can block a salesperson from looking objectively at what is going on in a situation and can often make them miss out on picking up vital clues, such as signs of an interested prospect. Fear makes people play in defence mode, and when you do anything with a defensive mindset, you tend to make yourself smaller. I will use a boxing analogy to explain this better. When a fighter gets hit then, he becomes defensive, to protect his body and face. When this happens, the fighter is communicating to his opponent through his body language that he is focusing on not getting punched rather than doing the punching. So, when he gets knocked out it wasn't necessarily the final punch. It was more to do with the fearful way he had acted in the preceding minutes, which came about from having fear enter his mind.

One key thing to do is rationalise your fears. You need to know exactly what your fears are in order to address them. Change your perspective on fear. If you just try to fight it head-on, then you will experience tension. Make fear your friend, not your enemy. Remember that fear is there to protect us and not harm us. It's a bit like a meddling parent that means well but is interfering too much. So, once we switch our perspective, we can consciously decide to perform despite the existence of fear. Once we shift the way fear exists in our mind, this will change the biological chemicals of fear felt in the body. Fear magnifies the shock value of a punch in your mind because it will get you to focus more on what you fear. The more you focus on this negative outcome, the more you will believe it to be true, even before it happens. Furthermore, the more you focus on a fearful/ negative outcome, the more you automatically lose focus on the winning outcome.

People have many fears. I've selected a few that I believe are common for salespeople, sales leaders and entrepreneurs.

Fear of performing to less than your potential. This can be a good fear to have.

This allows you to fully dive into what you want to accomplish and allows you to positively push yourself. Having this fear often makes you try to develop yourself. If you are in sales, then this can help you to make the decision to invest in yourself, in order to achieve your full potential. To conquer this fear (and make it work for you), you must fully accept that there is a possibility that you might come up short. However, by accepting it, you stop fighting the possibility of failure and end up fully engaging in it. This makes you fully focused and less likely to be distracted, which in turn makes it less likely that you will fail.

Fear of failure – This is arguably the most common fear, especially when it comes to people who are involved in the world of sales. It is understandable to feel this, as our entire lives have been built around being rewarded for success. When we were at school, we were rewarded for good grades and reprimanded for bad ones by our teacher. We were further rewarded and reprimanded by our parents for success or failure. Therefore, from a young age, we learnt to fear the consequences of failure. As adults, this continues and in fact, magnifies, as we have even more examples of pain when we failed in our minds. However, an excessive fear of failure can have a negative effect on our chances of success.

Take the example of an entrepreneur who is worried that they won't hit their sales revenues and as a result might need to close down their business. In this case, you would say they have a high fear of failure. The likelihood is that they would take this energy into meetings that they have with clients. As a result, when they are talking to clients they are likely to come across as anxious, timid and pushy. This is likely to have the opposite effect of what they want. It could turn the client off, and the chances of the sale will diminish. This is exactly what happened to me in the story that I recounted earlier, in which I was required to sell to the CEO and needed the deal to keep my job. I had a lot at stake and therefore felt a strong fear of failure. I went into the meeting with a high level of anxiety and was timid in my approach. I even lied to the CEO as I didn't know the answer and was too scared to admit it. This resulted in the meeting going the worst possible way it could have and me blowing the sale.

Furthermore, when we have a fear of failure, we are automatically implanting into our subconscious brains a seed that there is the possibility that we will fail. The more we worry, the more this seed grows. Additionally, we emit negative energy to our clients that is not beneficial to gaining a sale.

So how do we go about reducing our fear of failure? How do we use it to our advantage? The first thing to remember is that, as with most things, there are healthy and unhealthy levels. Eating fish is healthy for you but if eaten excessively it can cause Mercury poisoning. Working hard is good, but when done excessively it can lead to burnout etc. It's the same with our fears. Having a degree of fear of failure can be good, as it forces us to take action in order to avoid pain. It motivates us to try harder and develop ourselves further. However, if we are too afraid, we experience anxiety, timidness, negativity and stress.

I make this point so that you don't beat yourself up for having a small amount of fear of failure. A small amount is healthy.

So, let's get on to the matter of actually reducing it. Firstly, you should avoid making it all-encompassing and stop catastrophizing. Don't think of whatever you're trying to achieve as the be-all and end-all. The reality is that it isn't as bad as it seems. For example, if we refer back to my previous story of when I desperately needed the sale, at that time, I believed that I needed the sale to keep my job. If I got sacked, I wouldn't be able to afford my rent and so on. The reality was that I didn't get sacked, and even if I had, there were plenty of other jobs (and my savings) to fall back on. In my mind, I had blown it out of proportion, and this resulted in me feeling even more fearful.

Secondly, you should not let it define you.

It's good to have a burning desire to achieve an outcome, but not to let it define you or your worth. In my case, at the time of my disastrous meeting, I felt that if I failed, I would be considered a sales failure. I thought that I wasn't good enough if the meeting didn't go according to plan. I thought that if the meeting didn't go well, that meant that I didn't belong in a sales career. I was letting the possibility of failure in that one particular meeting (and in that particular job to some extent) define me as a salesperson. When I did that, I increased my anxiety around failing as I had made it all-encompassing.

The next step in reducing your fear of failure is to look at the wider picture. When we are afraid of failing at something, we are often looking at it with tunnel vision. For example, we might be afraid of losing out on a big deal. The thought that will run through our mind will be 'I will lose out on much-needed revenue, I will lose out on much-needed commission, I will be reprimanded by my boss' etc. However, if we looked at the situation in its entirety, then we might see that there are benefits of going after this deal, whatever the outcome. It could be that as a result of trying to close this big deal, we are learning a lot more about selling to a particular type of client. Or that we are learning new sales skills that we will need to make this kind of deal happen. Perhaps it's that we are building a relationship with a senior buyer in a leading company. When we focus on the overall picture, then we gain more perspective. We start to think that whatever the outcome is, we will still benefit and gain something. This helps us to manage the anxiety around the situation and reduce our fear of failure.

One of the most effective ways of reducing the fear of failure is to not think about it. I don't mean ignore it or pretend everything is ok. I mean to focus our minds elsewhere. Instead, we can focus our minds on the possibility of victory. We can imagine what that would look like, how that would feel, sound, and taste like (use all of our five senses), when we fill our minds with what success looks like, we do two things. First of all, it makes us feel better and take more positive actions, which usually result in more success. Secondly, we stop thinking about failure and, as a result, are far less likely to experience it. When I have suggested this to my clients, many of them have said they focus on success rather than failure. A good way of testing to see if this is true is to close your eyes and think about the outcome you are looking for (close an important deal, make your business a success etc). Then notice what bodily sensation you are feeling and where it's located. If you feel a nervous feeling in the pit of your stomach, then it's likely that you are focusing more on the possibility of failure than the possibility of victory. If, however, you feel your heart area open up and expand, then you are more likely to feel confident and focus on the possibility of victory.

Fear of being judged – This is another common fear among people. Understandably, many of us have this fear as we have evolved with it. Thousands of years ago, when we all lived in tribes, it was very important for our basic survival that we remained part of the tribe. If we did something that the rest of the tribe judged as bad, then we were likely to be excluded from it. When we were on our own, our chances of survival became very limited. So, we have evolved with a genuine fear of being judged. However, although the reality in our modern life is that a negative judgement will not result in our death, we are social creatures and don't like to look bad in the eyes of others. Furthermore, the modern equivalent of being shunned from the tribe is losing a key customer or losing our job.

Fear of judgement can be confused with fear of failure. However, they are two different fears. Fear of failure is being scared of not achieving what you set out to. Fear of judgement is being scared of what people will think of us or how we will be perceived if we don't achieve an outcome or we get something wrong. In fact, when we think we are afraid of failure we are just as likely to be afraid of the criticism or judgement that we will receive because of it.

The first thing that we can do to reduce our fear of judgement, is to realise that the likelihood of being judged is less than we think. Most people are too busy and have their own set of problems to be busy judging you. Just remembering that simple fact can relieve a lot of the pressure.

It is also very useful to concentrate on our bigger mission or outcome, and this can also help reduce our fear of failure. When our thoughts are more attached to our higher vision, we are less likely to care about what others think of us. For example, my ultimate mission is to educate and empower millions of people globally so that they can maximise their potential and hit peak performance. Every time I am afraid of doing something, I remember this mission, and it lifts me out of fear and into positive action. Your mission doesn't have to be so grand. It could be something as simple as wanting to win an award for the best salesperson in your company that year. As long as it inspires you to leave your fear behind you, then use it.

Often, when we are selling, we are worried about how our customers will perceive or judge us. We may try to impress them, and this makes us tense and unauthentic. However, if we forget about impressing them and focus on how best we can serve them, then we take the pressure off ourselves. Our thoughts shift from 'How can I persuade this customer to like me and buy from me?' to 'How can I best serve this customer so they get the result they want?' Doing this makes the customer see us in a favourable light. Additionally, we end up being more authentic as we are only looking to serve them as opposed to impressing them. Finally, thinking this way takes us out of a fearful energy and into a more positive space.

The fear of letting go - An often misunderstood fear is our fear of letting go. Many people will casually announce, 'I am a control freak, I always need to be on top of everything, and I hate not knowing what's going on.' There is nothing wrong with this mentality, and a lot of the time, it's a good thing. However, when it comes to sales it can negatively affect our results. This is because focusing on maintaining control makes it difficult to let go. We need to know what the customer is thinking, what the team we are managing are doing, which other vendors the customer is speaking with etc. We are not able to sit in peace and this creates an inner anxiety that is likely to affect our decision-making and actions negatively, possibly costing us a deal or a staff member. Sometimes we need to swallow the fear and have the confidence to simply let go. Try your best and then trust yourself and others around you to come through. Letting go does not mean not caring or not taking action. Zen philosophy states that letting go is to lose attachment to the outcome. This means that we still put in our full effort but don't get emotionally attached to the outcome. In letting go, we feel empowered, as we are in a more relaxed state from which we can make better decisions. In one of the companies, I used to work in, the sales manager would get one sales rep to close another rep's deal if he thought that the rep was too attached to the outcome. The fact that the rep was too attached and unable to let go, meant he was likely to scupper the deal.

Letting go of the need for control, or the fear of a particular outcome not happening the way in which we want can be powerful. Ironically, by doing this we actually gain more control and better results without trying too hard.

In summary, our fears are there to protect us but we often indulge in them excessively. The key is to keep them minimised and as a result, take more positive action. This is especially important in the world of sales, where action is king. I have often found that this is an area that is overlooked. Companies will spend millions of pounds to have their sales teams trained in the latest sales techniques, but if they don't know how to manage their fears (or even are unaware of their fears), then no amount of sales training will be effective. If I were to use an analogy, it would be like sending a soldier into battle with a gun, even though the soldier was too afraid to fire it.

That strategy would not produce a very effective soldier!

Chapter 6

Get laser focused

When I did some of my best work and had my best results in sales (and in life in general), I had been in a state of complete focus. In the sports world, they call this flow state. I cannot express too much just how important it is to be laser-focused. The problem with today's society is that we have far too many distractions. A lot of this is due to technology, which means that we have a never-ending flow of information coming our way. We are always connected and know what is happening with different people and about different places in the world. Not only can this become mentally fatiguing, but it can also lead us to be constantly chasing shiny new objects which prevent us from putting all our time, thought and energy into any one thing at a time. If you think of all the people who have achieved great things, they have all focused on one major goal at a time.

Steve Jobs became obsessed with creating the iPhone. Warren Buffet was obsessed with learning about investing. He read all the books, attended all the seminars and consumed as much knowledge as he could about different companies, he thought were good to invest in. Furthermore, he learnt all he could about historical investors and the art of investing. He didn't simultaneously create a business that sold products or services, work on becoming a renowned public speaker and start learning about and investing in real estate. In the beginning, he focused on one thing only. INVESTING! Once he had mastered that, he moved on to other things. By doing this, he massively increased his chances of success, as he was able to devote all his energy to one thing. This might sound obvious, but it surprises me how people who are looking to become successful pursue multiple passions and interests simultaneously.

When it comes to sales the same is true. I have seen companies and their teams pursue multiple sales strategies at once. I have seen them pursue one strategy and then, if it didn't get immediate results, abandon it. I have seen individuals do the same.

So what does laser focus look like when selling?

1. **Focussing on one major goal at any one time.** For example, if you were a business owner and wanted to double your sales that month, that would mean that 80% of your energy should go into bringing in immediate sales or opportunities. If you also wanted to write a report that you would use as a sales generation tool, that would have to wait. If you wanted to bring in a big client that you had some traction with, but which you knew

would be likely to take a few months to bring in, then you would need to de-prioritise that particular deal. If you wanted to start your podcast, that would have to wait. Most people would say that you need to keep lots of plates spinning at once in order to be successful. I think that is true only to a certain extent and, more often than not, it hampers the chance of a successful outcome. If you are going to spin plates, then those plates should all be aligned with your major goal. So, in the example above, it would have to be related to doubling your revenue that month. People who become involved in pursuing different goals or targets at one time are likely to end up not achieving their primary outcome

2. **Focus on only one activity at a time.** This point is similar to the one above but is more about the individual tasks you do throughout the day. For example, if you are a salesperson who decides to spend the morning cold calling, then you must only focus on that one task. Do not check your emails or take incoming calls from someone, and don't get dragged into a meeting (unless you have to). According to research, it takes 23 minutes for us to get refocused once we have become distracted. So, imagine you planned to undertake three hours of cold calling one morning, but after 30 minutes, you checked your emails and read one that was important and which took time and energy to respond to. Additionally, it contained news that made

you feel a little anxious, for example, concerning a customer threatening to leave. Not only would it take up to 23 minutes of your morning to refocus, but you would return to cold calling in a negative and anxious state. This would have a big impact on your cold-calling slot. Then imagine you also replied to a WhatsApp message, allowed yourself to get dragged into a five-minute meeting and replied to yet another email. Whilst you might think that these tasks only take a few minutes, the distraction they would cause would have a big impact on your cold-calling results. If you allowed this to happen on a regular basis, you would see a major effect on your performance.

3. **Practice mindfulness** – Mindfulness is a mental state achieved by focusing your awareness on the present moment. It's about living very much in the now and it has gained a lot of traction in the last few years. However, a lot of what has been written has been based on how it can reduce stress and increase well-being (which it does). I also find that it can have a massive impact on productivity and performance. In particular, it can help with your focus. As a sales-person when you are relaxed, focused and present, then you are less likely to feel any emotion. We feel emotion when we live in the past or the future. Our minds can easily wander throughout every minute of the day. Imagine if you were writing a sales email and whilst doing it your

mind wandered back to a difficult client conversation that you had the day before (negative emotion). Or it wandered and dwelt on the possibility of you losing the client (negative emotion). If you had been present and purely focused on the email you were writing, then not only would you have completed the email a lot quicker but it would be devoid of negative emotion and much more likely to be an effective sales email. Practising mindfulness can help you do that. The following quick and simple exercise can help with this:

Sit down in your chair and close your eyes. Then mentally scan your body, starting from your head, working your way down your face and body, all the way to your toes. Just pay attention to how each body part feels. Don't judge it as good or bad, but focus purely on how it feels (is it stiff, loose, warm, cold etc). Do this for several minutes a few times a day. You will find that, over time, you will get better and better at it, and eventually, it will help you to become focused. This will translate into your day-to-day work so that, eventually, you will become far better focused on living in the present and focusing on the task at hand. I used to be someone who had a terrible concentration span and would often get distracted and unfocused. I believe this one practice has had the biggest impact on my ability to concentrate and focus intensely. Becoming mindful allows you to stay in the present, which in turn allows you to remain emotionally unaffected and focused. Ultimately, this leads to greater productivity and, eventually more sales.

Chapter 7

Develop a winning attitude

Success in any discipline, including sales, is affected by your attitude. For me, an entrepreneur, sales leader or salesperson who has the right attitude will even beat someone who is technically superior to them. What makes a great attitude? This is made up of many attributes including those already covered in this book.

A winning mind-set – Some people who play to win and others play merely to take part. I do not believe that children should get awards merely for taking part in school. Sales and business are competitive environments and should be played with the spirit of playing to win. This does not mean that it can't be playful or fun. Neither does it mean that playing to win means trampling over the competition or cheating clients purely for the sake of winning. What I mean by playing to win is that you must look to beat yourself every single day. Beat your performance from the day before, beat your previous results, beat the demons that come into your mind and demand the very best from yourself. When you do this, then you will naturally win the sales (and life) game.

Many people think they have a winning mindset, but if they are honest with themselves, they don't. They do not want to leave their comfort zone. They won't have difficult conversations, they don't want to spend money to invest in themselves and they won't make certain sacrifices. They won't do all of these things despite knowing that doing them will help them achieve their goals. They are playing simply to take part and not to win. They will say that they tried their best and gave it all they could, but the reality is they didn't. If you are working for a company in the sales team, or if you are running your own business, then I believe you absolutely must play to win every day. This also includes giving your absolute best to your customers. Your customers should be the most important people in your life (from a business perspective). You also have a duty to your colleagues, employees, bosses and everyone else that you come across to become the very best version of yourself. Playing to win is for yourself, but it is just as much for those around you.

Another aspect of a winning mindset is to dominate. However, this does not mean dominating others, as many would think a winning mindset would mean. Yes, it's important not to be dominated by others, to stand your ground and to have some very clear boundaries. However, for me, true domination is when you dominate your mind. As I have highlighted before in this book, our minds is wired to keep us safe. When we are in safety mode, we tend to be in the mindset of playing to take part; therefore, it is very important that we take control of our minds. When you have a career in sales, you must regularly ask yourself if you are playing it big or small. Is your mind making you play it safe or on your side and playing to win? When we have a negative thought such as ' I don't think that this deal is going to happen unless I lower the price' or 'I don't think my product or service is good enough for this customer to want to purchase', then we must immediately go about silencing that thought. The longer we let it stay in our minds, the more it grows and the more doubtful we become. Don't even give it the chance to grow; crush it as soon as it enters your mind. Though this is easier said than done, it can be achieved with practice. Some of the tools that I mentioned earlier in this book, such as affirmations, can help us. However, I find the most effective tool is to remember to dominate the thought, to remember to extinguish it as soon as it enters your mind. If you do this over a period of weeks, months and years, eventually your brain will automatically learn to have that response. So that the next time you are in front of a client and are playing it small due to fear, your mind will take over and crush the thought. Your mind will then be free to play to win.

The final aspect of a winning mind-set is based on never giving up. There is an old saying that says 'It's not over until it's over'. You need to keep high levels of resilience in order to foster a winning mindset. Resilience tends to come through overcoming tough situations. The more you overcome, the more battle-hardened you become. Resilience can be something that you actively work on as well. Firstly, you should connect to your higher mission/purpose as this will keep you going strong in the face of adversity.

Secondly, make a promise to yourself that you won't fold or give up. If you're in a sales role or a business owner, then make a promise that however bad your sales results get, you won't quit the game. Too many people don't make that commitment and they quit after experiencing a lean time.

Another way to stop yourself from giving up is to limit the options available to you. Generally speaking, options are a good thing to have in life but they can be a double-edged sword, and can create weakness in the mind. Sometimes a plan b (or even c and d) can hamper our success. The following story is a well-known one, and I think demonstrates the point well.

In 1519 Hernan Cortes and his 600 men arrived on the shores of the New World. Upon arrival, he ordered his men to burn the ships. By doing this, he sent a clear message to them all that there was no turning back, and the only way they could get back would be through conquest. Whilst this might be an extreme example, it still is a very relevant one. Having a backup plan can mean we don't put all our efforts into our main plan. We don't become resolute enough to ensure that our main plan succeeds at all costs. When we are fully committed to our main plan, giving up is no longer an option. This, in turn, helps us to develop a winning mindset. So next time you have a stiff sales target or a sales challenge, commit to not giving up until it's solved. In fact, discount altogether the option of it not getting solved. If you say to yourself, 'I have to solve this, no matter what,' then you are more likely to generate the resources needed to get the result.

A winning mentality is very important in all high-performance professions. If you think of all of the highest performers in sports (Tiger Woods, Michael Jordan, Christiano Ronaldo) and in business (Henry Ford, Steve Jobs, Elon Musk), they all share a winning mindset. They were not just taking part to make up the numbers but were taking part to win. Carry that mindset into your sales!

Chapter 8

The voices within

One of the books that changed my whole way of thinking is called The Inner Game of Tennis by Tim Gallwey. The book explains how achieving success in the game of tennis (or any area of success) is mainly a result of the internal dialogue you have with yourself. The better the dialogue, the better your results. The teachings from the book have formed the basis of a lot of my coaching work.

One concept explored by this book is that people are formed of two parts: the I and Myself. People will often say they are talking to themselves, but who exactly is this 'I' and who is the 'Myself'? The book explains that these are effectively two separate entities within us. Professor Steve Peters outlines a similar concept in his book 'The Chimp Paradox.' There are many other books that explore the idea of two entities, including the ego and the self. The self is thought of as our true being at its most pure. The ego is the mental construct in our mind that often interfere.

I am a believer in the concept of two entities or two voices that play within our heads. When it comes to success, I believe that there is a voice that helps us and the voice that hinders us. For the purposes of this book, let's call those voices 'The Devil and 'The Angel'.

The voice of the Devil is our critical and negative self-voice, the one that will often berate us when we get things wrong. The one that is unforgiving and tends to focus on our weaknesses and blows them out of proportion. The one that tells us why we aren't good enough to achieve something and all that could go wrong. The Devil can also be the voice that is delusional and has a sense of self-grandeur. It gives us an unrealistic sense of ourselves and a situation and makes us believe that we are greater than we are. The Angel is the complete opposite. It will remind us of what we are great at, why we deserve success, praise us, highlight our strengths etc. Often both voices can be playing in our heads at the same time. If we listen to the Devil too much, then we will become nervous, unconfident and negative or the complete opposite, where we are overconfident and narcissistic. This way, we hamper our chances of success. The key is to listen and have a healthy respect for them both. However, we should believe the words of the Angel a lot more than the words of the Devil.

Let's apply this to a sales situation. Imagine that you have just completed a cold call with a client. The call didn't go the way you hoped it would and you feel a little dejected. At that point the Devil might be saying, 'You really messed that one up, you're so stupid, why couldn't you remember your cold calling training? Everyone in the office just heard you mess that up and probably thinks that you are not cut out for sales. Maybe you should just give up.' The negative judgements of the Devil are likely to make you do one of two things. You are either going to reduce the number of cold calls you make, or you will carry on with negative thoughts going through your head. Either way, your chances of success are minimal.

The Devil might have a different response, though, and say something along the lines of. 'Who does that client think they are? They are being so stupid in rejecting my offer! That was a brilliant sales pitch and the reason they didn't want to move forward is that they didn't get the offer.' In this case, the Devil is putting all the blame on the client. It's making you think that the reason the client doesn't want to buy is that there is something wrong with them. By listening to this message from the Devil, you are less likely to look for ways to improve. You are more likely to sound condescending or arrogant when you speak on the phone, and ultimately, you are less likely to have the outcomes that you want.

Let's say, that after the cold call you chose to listen to the voice of the Angel. It might be saying, 'Don't worry, not everyone is going to want to buy from you. Keep trying, remember the last deal you made came on the back of a cold call. You're a step closer to another sale. That was one tough customer and you handled that as best you could.'

In this situation, you have taken the negative judgement of yourself and others out of the equation. The more positive (but still very neutral) judgements of the Angel should ensure that you keep making cold calls and, when you do, then you will feel far more positive when making them. At the same time, you will keep looking for ways to improve without judging yourself as wrong, or a failure for things that need improving. This will ultimately result in you making more sales.

So how do you ensure that you listen to the Angel more than you listen to the Devil? This is not an easy thing to do and in fact, it is far easier and more natural to listen to the Devil than to the Angel. There are two reasons for this. Firstly, human nature tends to listen and focus on the negative rather than the positive. Our brains have evolved that way as a survival technique.

Secondly, we are far more comfortable when we have something or someone to blame when things don't go our way, even if that means we are blaming ourselves. Blame and judgement go hand in hand, and the Devil loves them both.

So, the first step in making the voice of the Angel louder is to make the voice of the Devil smaller. In order to do this, we must stop judging. Think of an umpire officiating a tennis or cricket match. The umpire is not a player, a fan or a commentator. Their job is not to deem something good or bad, their job is just to observe what is going on. If a cricket umpire sees that a bowler has overstepped the crease when delivering a ball, then he will say it's a no-ball. He will not judge the bowler in any way. He won't tell the bowler that he is wrong and needs to work on his delivery. He will simply observe and make his call. So we must first look to observe ourselves and our performance and not judge. Once we do this, then we are able to see things for what they really are. We stop exaggerating things or blowing them out of proportion. We see things in a more neutral and correct state.

We also have to work on making the voice of the Angel louder.

This is a suitable point to introduce some of the concepts of Neuro-Linguistic Programming (NLP). NLP is a huge topic to cover, but it's relevant to helping us change our thoughts. In essence, NLP is about how we communicate with ourselves. One of the key concepts of NLP is Modalities. Modalities are related to our five senses, (visual, auditory, kinaesthetic, olfactory, and gustatory) that we use to make sense of the world around us. When we are thinking about something we are often using one (or more) of the five senses. Most people will predominantly use visual and auditory. We can use our modalities when it comes to changing our thoughts and feelings. We can use them when we want to make the Angel dominant over the Devil. Below is a little exercise that can be used to do this:

Imagine that we are finding the voice of our Devil in precedence after an unsuccessful sales call. This is where we can use a NLP tool called the screen of the mind technique to make changes.

Close your eyes and take several deep breaths in and out of the nose. Get yourself into a relaxed state with as clear a mind as possible. Next, go through the process of creating two movies in your mind. In one screen take your present situation. You see an image of yourself looking dejected after a cold call. You hear the voice of judgement criticising you for not handling the call well, you see and hear a negative scene. It's like you're watching a bad movie about yourself. With this movie put a dark frame around the movie screen. Next, make another mental movie in your mind. However, in this movie you see an image of you looking content with yourself after a sales call. You see that it went well and that you did your very best. In the movie you hear others around you telling you how well it went and how they learnt a thing or two listening to you make the call. You hear yourself accepting the congratulations with pleasure. In summary, you see and hear a very positive movie of a sales call going well. With this mental movie, put a bright gold frame around the movie screen.

Next, you must make the negative movie as large as you can in your mind's eye. Make the images big, bright and bold. Make the negative voices as loud as possible and capture how you feel when you are seeing this movie. You are likely to feel very negative watching it. Don't fight those feelings or try to ignore them. Fully embrace them, but don't judge yourself for feeling them. Once you have a clear movie with the sounds, images and feelings, start making it all smaller and quieter. Shrink the image of the movie in your mind. Shrink it to a postage stamp size and place it on the corner of a page. Next, mute the sound that is coming from all the characters in the movie (including what you are saying to yourself). After that, start to detach from the feelings by becoming an observer rather than a character in the movie who wouldn't take on the negative feelings.

Next, take the mental image of the positive version of the movie and repeat the same process. Make the images bigger, the colours brighter, the sounds louder and fully embrace the positive images. Then, repeat the process of reversing all that and making the image into a postage stamp-size, on the opposite side of the page as the postage stamp of the negative movie. The final part of the process is to take the positive (postage stamp-sized) image and mentally watch it expand and smash through the negative (postage stamp-sized) image. Do this several times and, each time you do it, experience the feeling of breaking through your negativity. Feel as if the Angel is destroying the Devil in you. This might sound a little strange, but it's a powerful NLP technique. When it's done properly, and several times over, it can be a really powerful way of making the Angel dominate the Devil. You will find that, over a period of time, your Devil will appear less often, and your Angel will become dominant.

There are other techniques you can use to make the Devil smaller and less significant and make the Angel bigger and more significant, and I could devote a whole book to the subject. However, this summary should be sufficient to enable anyone to start the process. I would highly recommend that you use the techniques that I have explained above on a regular basis.

Controlling our Devil and feeding our Angel is one of the most important things we can do if we want to achieve high performance. What and how we think is a huge factor in the success of the actions we take. Ultimately it affects the results that we get.

Chapter 9

Bring on the joy.

It's a well-known fact that the happier, more inspired and motivated you are, together with having low-stress levels, the more you will sell. However, despite knowing this, the majority of salespeople, teams and entrepreneurs will continue to sell in a very stressful and pressurised way.

When I worked in the corporate world, I would often hear sales managers make comments such as, 'Pressure is good, pressure creates diamonds.' Once I overheard a manager saying 'The teams are starting to do well now, let's make sure we keep up the pressure on them so that we don't lose momentum.' My belief is that applying pressure is not the best way to create results. People often confuse pressure with taking action and think that pressure will make people take action. Whilst this is true, it will often cause them to take the wrong type of action. It often causes people to make poor choices, act irrationally and become stressed.

In contrast, it is much more productive to cultivate inspired action, especially if you're a sales leader.

People will take far more action (and more positive action) if they are feeling inspired as opposed to pressure. It is also beneficial to introduce more playful action to what we do. Children become occupied for hours at a time with activities because they are playing. They do not worry about the result and therefore put no pressure on themselves. We could benefit from bringing this childlike energy and play to our sales because we are less likely to feel pressure and more likely to have fun. When we are having fun, we are more likely to feel inspired and, due to the extra endorphins that our brain sends, more likely to feel relaxed and confident and take better actions.

So how can we include more fun and play in our sales? For a start, we must not confuse having the playful energy of a child with being childlike in our communication and actions. For if we act like children, then, of course, we will look unprofessional, and that will hamper our results and performance. Bringing play to our sales means a few things:

1. **Detach yourself from the end result.** Whilst this might sound contradictory to being attached to your vision/ mission and being goal-oriented, it actually isn't. We must constantly keep our end vision/ mission in our mind and being goal-oriented is good. However, we want to detach from the outcome with our day-to-day sales activity and deals. When we do this, we tend to feel

less anxious and desperate about the result. Consequently, we tend to have more fun undertaking the activities and ironically, we are more likely to achieve success. Another way of detaching from an outcome is to focus on the process. Focus on working a process and bring joy to that. In a sales situation, this would mean enjoying the process of finding out and getting to know about a customer, as opposed to focusing on whether or not they will buy from you.

2. **Look to empower as opposed to impress** – When we make other people around us feel secure, good and empowered, we tend to feel happier ourselves. This is the same with our clients. A couple of years ago, a client came to me and said that he wanted to impress his clients when he sold to them. He felt that his clients were not always very impressed by him and sometimes he felt that he didn't have enough gravitas with them. I told him to do one thing from then on. I told him to stop focusing on impressing his clients and to focus more on serving them and making them feel good and empowered. He found that once he started to do that, he stopped stressing so much about what they thought about him and as a result started to have more fun in his interactions with them. Ultimately, this made him get his desired result of increased gravitas. We should take this spirit to interactions that we have with all people,

including our bosses, colleagues, workers and clients.

3. **Bring curiosity and wonder to all we do**: Let's take the example of Albert Einstein. Einstein was a genius, but he also wanted to achieve great things. However, one of his greatest assets was that he approached his work with an almost childlike curiosity and wonder. He was more interested in exploring the answer to something than the result of what he was looking for. In fact, he said that he would often (like most scientists) stumble upon a discovery whilst looking for an answer to an unrelated question. This curiosity and wonder made him very successful at what he did and one of the greatest scientists of all time. Bringing curiosity and wonder to your sales (understanding your clients, learning about sales, overcoming problems etc.) will make you develop more playful energy, which in turn will help you bring more joy to what you do. Ultimately it will make you more inspired, productive and effective.

The inner game summarised.

The first part of this book has focused on people developing their inner game in order to maximise their performance. This is a very important part of the book, as I truly believe that high performance and success ultimately depend on the relationship that we have with ourselves, our internal dialogue, controlling our fears and connecting to our deeper values and vision.

The first step is to become self-aware of who we are, what we want and why we want it. By doing this, we are able to keep ourselves motivated and more resilient when we hit the roadblocks that we inevitably face.

We then want to create powerful goals that are set from a deeper and more emotional place than just our logical mind. Doing this makes them more meaningful for us, which in turn will keep us motivated and less likely to give up.

We need to keep ourselves focused and limit the distractions we face. Doing this makes us disciplined and means that we devote our time and energy to our goals. When we do this, we stop time and energy wasters from robbing us. We add fuel to the fire rather than take the fuel away.

We need to control our fears and limiting beliefs. It's important that we recognise and accept them but don't let them become all-encompassing. Furthermore, we need to train ourselves to act with courage and take positive action despite our fears.

We simultaneously need to feed our confidence and self-belief. We need to remind ourselves of our successes and focus more on how and why we will achieve our goals as opposed to why things won't work out.

We should gain a good understanding of where our beliefs have come from and work out which of them are serving us and which are taking us away from where we want to get to; which are empowering and which are disempowering.

We should learn how to control our minds and reduce the noise of our negative voices or inner critic. We want to feed our more positive self-talk. Doing this, again, helps us to remain confident and take positive action.

We also need to remember to bring joy to what we do. Focus more on the process as opposed to the result and learn to detach ourselves from the result. Doing this will ironically help us to achieve what we set out to do.

As sales professionals, leaders or entrepreneurs it's important that we focus on developing our inner game (and that of our teams) even more so than our outer skills and strategies. This is because doing this allows us to build a rock-solid base, a foundation that we can build on to become more successful.

However, we do need to build our sales skills too, and the next section of the book focuses on that. We focus on what I believe to be the key sales skills that we need to develop, to improve performance and get the results that we desire.

Chapter 10

It's all in the questions

The quality of the results that we achieve in sales depends largely on the types of questions that we ask our clients. There is a famous saying in the sales world which is 'telling isn't selling.' One big mistake that salespeople and entrepreneurs make when selling is to go into tell mode. By this, I mean that they tell their customers what their problems are, they tell their customers why they need help, and they tell their customers how they will help them. They do all this without fully understanding the nature of the customer's problem, challenge or aspiration. When selling, I encourage my clients to think of themselves as doctors who are trying to find out about a patient's problems before diagnosing a solution. You wouldn't expect to walk into your doctor's surgery and immediately hear his or her opinion about your problem, why you have it and what medicine you should take to fix it. You would expect to answer some questions about your problem, how long it has persisted, how it is affecting you etc. The same approach should be taken when you're selling anything.

There are lots of questioning methodologies that can be used in sales. These are a few of them:

- Problem resolution questions
- Agitation questions
- Solution and feeling-based questions
- Needs-based questions
- Objection testing questions
- Yes/ No questions
- Open questions
- Level 1, 2 and 3 questions

Here we will focus on open questions and level 1, 2 and 3 questions.

Open questions – Open questions are questions that cannot be answered with a simple yes or no. They begin with

- Who
- What
- When
- Where
- Why

They help us to better understand a customer and see things from their perspective, as you get feedback in their own words instead of stock answers. Furthermore, they get the customer talking. Generally speaking, people like to hear the sound of their voice and don't like to be spoken at. Open questions encourage clients to open up and express themselves. Here are a few examples of open questions

- What is the main challenge you are facing in your business right now?
- When are you looking to implement sales training?
- Who else are you speaking to when it comes to addressing your training needs?
- Where are you looking to expand your business?
- Why are you looking to expand into those territories?

Asking open questions is especially important in the initial stages of a sales conversation as they give you a good overall understanding of the situation the customer is facing. They open up the breadth of the conversation and allow you to structure the subsequent conversations on the back of them. I also find that asking good open questions gets the customer to think about their situation better and sometimes makes them uncover something they never thought of.

Follow up questions

The concept of asking open questions has been known for a long time and many people employ this strategy when selling nowadays. However, I often find that they seem to be asking these questions for the sake of asking them. They have received some training or read that it's important, so they ask the question but then fail to follow up on the answer the customer gives them. The magic is often in the follow-up, for it is the answers to these questions that help you understand a customer and their needs better. Below is a concept that helps with follow-up questions:

Level 1, 2 and 3 questions

The concept of level 1,2 and 3 questions are based on the fact that people are like lasagne, as in they have multiple layers to them. When selling, it's your job to unpack those layers just as you would eat through each layer of a lasagne. So, what are these levels?

Level 1 questions are preliminary questions that initiate a conversation by revealing thoughts, facts, behaviours and situations. They are the foundation questions that help you get a basic understanding of the customer and are best used at the start of a conversation with buyers.

They expose only rudimentary information, and they don't help the salesperson get an in-depth understanding of the buyer. Level 1 questions typically answer the questions What? Who? and When?

Examples include –

- What are your department goals this quarter?
- What percentage of the market do you currently have?

- What is your current sales situation?
- What is your budget?
- How many other vendors are you considering?
- What is it that you're looking for in a vendor?

I have found that many salespeople stop after asking a level one question, or they focus all of their questions on level 1 only.

Level 2 questions – Once you ask your first layer questions, you will have a basic understanding of the customer's requirements. So now it's time to get to the next layer and understand those requirements in a bit more detail. These questions are important as they help prospective customers to think more about their situation and to synthesise information. They often ask customers to either assess or explain a level 1 response.

Examples include -

- Why is that a department goal?
- Why are you looking for those things in a vendor?
- What made you choose the vendors you're considering?
- How did you manage to get such a large market share?

Level 3 questions are the final layer. They are arguably the most important but aren't always asked. These questions usually address customers on an emotional or tactical level and the information that you get at this level can transform a sale. These questions usually help you to understand what a customer is hoping to move to and where they are planning to move away from. When you ask customers level 3 questions, you build a stronger relationship, and that helps them trust you.

Examples include –

- If your department's goal isn't reached, then what are the consequences?
- If the problem you described isn't resolved, then how will it impact your sales?
- If you choose the wrong vendor, then what impact would that have?
- How would you personally be affected if XYZ is resolved?

Level 3 questions tend to look at the consequences of something not happening. When you can help a customer to articulate the consequences of achieving or not achieving a goal, or the consequences of a problem being or not being resolved, then you are getting into their buying motives.

Here is a short example of level 1, 2 and 3 questions working together in a conversation

You: What is the number one challenge your business is currently facing? (Level 1).

Customer: We are not hitting our sales targets. In fact, we haven't done so for three consecutive quarters.

You: Why do you think that is? What's stopping you from doing this? (Level 2).

Customer: Our salespeople are not effective at closing deals. Many of them take a deal quite far but then are not able to get it over the line. Furthermore, when they do make the sale, they will often discount the price and therefore, our average order values have stayed pretty much the same for the last two years.

You: That sounds like a problem indeed. What are the consequences if more deals aren't closed, order values are not increased and the sales targets are missed next quarter? (Level 3).

Customer: It will probably mean that we have to release sales staff. To be honest with you, it will also mean that my job will be under pressure.

You can see in this short and simple example by asking the three levels of questions, you understand the depth of the problem. In this case, not hitting the sales target is a problem. However, the real problem is that people will lose their jobs (including the customer you're speaking with). Many salespeople will stop after asking a level 1 or maybe level 2 questions, by doing that they are missing out on the most significant details.

One key thing when asking open questions (in fact any time you're questioning) is to avoid making it sound like an interrogation or interview. People will become defensive if you do this and are less likely to open up. This is also likely to break the rapport that you are trying to build. Some of the ways that you can make your questions sound more natural and part of a conversation are as follows:

Framing them – When you put some context behind a question, it gives your client an understanding of your justification for asking them. For example, you could say, 'I want to make sure I understand your needs and requirements so that I can see if we are the right fit to work together and so that I can recommend an appropriate service. In order to do this, I will need to ask you a few questions so that I get a better understanding of your requirements.'

By framing your question in this manner, you are getting the customer's permission to ask your questions. You are appealing to their self-interest in terms of why it would be beneficial for them to answer your questions, and you are also mentally preparing them to respond to your questions.

Mixing them up- Another way to avoid your questions sounding like an interrogation is to alternate asking questions and making statements or comments. For example, if you have asked a couple of consecutive open questions and the client has responded, then you can add a comment of your own like 'Ah, I see, it's interesting that you say that, as I find most of my clients feel the same way. In fact, one of my clients did XYZ in their business recently. By doing this, you don't sound like an interviewer.

Chapter 11

Remember to listen

For me, the two most important skills in sales (apart from those that are mindset related), are questioning and listening.

Listening is very underrated. Although they may be aware of the theory, I don't think many people who sell realise how powerful a great listener can be. I have found that, since I took up coaching, my listening skills have improved significantly and as a result, I became a much better salesperson. Becoming an effective listener won't just make you a better salesperson though; it will also make you a better partner, friend and family member. It can help you in all areas of life.

There is a powerful quote that says: 'Don't listen to respond but listen to understand'. I think this is so powerful because it captures what most people do when listening to another person speaking. Most of the time, when listening, salespeople will either

- Zone out of the conversation or mind wander

- Think about the response they are going to give

This takes away so much away from their ability to understand a customer's needs. Furthermore, a customer can pick up on this and will feel less special, ultimately increasing the likelihood of no sale. I believe the reason that people do this is due to fear. You might wonder how fear can be related to poor listening.

Let me explain:

Let's say you are in a conversation with a client and they are speaking. Let's also say that, at that time, you are not selling much and really need the sale. Perhaps you're in two minds about what price to quote them. If your quote is too low, you will miss out on vital income, and if it is too high, you might scare them off. At the same time, a client who pulled out of a deal the week before might come to mind, and you worry about the same thing happening with the client you're currently talking to. With all these fearful thoughts taking your mind away from the present moment, your listening skills become severely diminished.

It is also possible that you are thinking about the best way to respond to your client rather than really listening to them. This can also be based on fear, as you are trying to impress them so that they buy from you. You want to make sure you give them the perfect response. So even though you are listening to what they are telling you, you are not doing it from the perspective of understanding them but more from the perspective of responding to them. The best way to listen effectively is to practise active listening. By active listening, I mean to listen to your client with undivided attention, to listen to them with all your mind and heart. To make sure that you are really trying to understand them, that you are trying to walk in their shoes, and that you are trying to feel what they are feeling.

The other part of active listening involves your facial expressions and body language. When your client is speaking to you, look into their eyes (not too intense, though as this can be disconcerting). Nod your head to demonstrate you're listening. Keep an open and warm body language. It's a good idea even to make some affirmative sounds such as 'um or aha'. When you do this, you make your customer feel more comfortable, and as a result, they open up more to you. This all might sound obvious, but you'll be surprised how many people don't do this. Their body is stiff, their faces expressionless, and they look somewhat robotic.

The other way to make yourself a great listener is to become curious and be more interested in helping them than selling to them. When this is the case, you will naturally want to listen to them as you will want to know their answer, not so you can sell to them, but because you want to help them. Furthermore, your client will notice this and will be more likely to open up and trust you. Often, it's a good idea not to think about any results when listening to a client but just to focus on what they need. We spoke previously about being focused and mindful when selling. This can especially help when you are listening to your client. You can effectively enter the listening zone!

Some people are naturally very good listeners, mainly for the reasons mentioned above. However, listening is a skill that can be cultivated. All it takes is a desire to understand your customer and practice listening to them.

Chapter 12

Tell me a story

In recent times there has been a lot of talk in the sales world about storytelling. I don't know why everyone is acting like it's such a new discovery when in fact it's something that has been important since the dawn of human communication.

Stories have been told throughout history, to not only entertain people but to also sell to them. Stories are effective because they

- Are interesting and engaging
- Usually connect with human emotions
- Are memorable
- Explain a journey

Ultimately humans are emotional. There is a famous saying that people buy with emotion and justify with logic. Stories help to resonate with the emotional part of them. So, what exactly is storytelling? Storytelling is when you explain the journey of you, your product, service or company. It's when you include what you do and why you do it. You explain the journey and explain the emotional reason behind it.

I'll give an example of a friend of mine who sells organic makeup products. These products use no endocrine disruptors, in other words, they don't use chemicals that damage our health. My friend also offers well-being courses and coaching as she believes in the power of natural and organic health. The reason my friend started her business was that her mother had a skin cancer scare a few years previously. It was a traumatic experience for my friend, and both she and her family went through an ordeal. Thankfully, her mother fought it off and was ok in the end.

The whole experience made my friend research skin cancer, and her research made her realise just how many modern-day products were bad for people's skin and health.

This experience made her quit her job and devote all her time, energy and attention to developing a makeup brand that used natural, clean products. It became a powerful motivator for her to create solutions that served the health of people in the world. She now runs a highly successful business

An important reason that she has become so successful and works with so many big brands is because of her story. Below I have written down two versions of how her product could be sold. One is with a story and one is without one.

The storyless version – Reborn Aura creates skin care products that do not contain endocrine disruptors. The products we use are 100% natural and organic. As a result, they do not pollute your skin or body. They are not only great for your health but also great for your skin. They have been made in laboratories that use the latest in dermatology techniques. This means our products are of the highest quality and keep you healthy from both the inside and outside.

The version with a story – Reborn Aura, was created because of the founder's love for human health. After her mother had a cancer scare which almost took her life, the founder researched skin cancer and, to her horror, discovered just how much the ingredients in many beauty products destroyed our health from the inside. It meant people were paying a heavy cost for their beauty. The founder was on a mission to create products that added to people's health rather than taking it away. Reborn Aura was created on the back of this. The products are 100% natural and do not contain harmful endocrine disruptors that have a detrimental effect on your health. Reborn Aura is all about creating products that make you beautiful from both the inside and the outside.

The above is a quick example of how adding a story can make a product or service come to life and become more appealing. Storytelling is an important subject on its own and could be covered in a separate book.

Another important part of selling is positioning. So, what exactly is positioning? For me, positioning is where your product or service stands in relation to other similar products or services in the market, as well as in the mind of the consumer.

I often find that this is not done optimally, especially when it comes to the smaller business owners that I work with. Many of them get too occupied in talking about the nuts and bolts of their product or their service and not enough about how they can help their customer. Let's take the following example:

Sarah runs a life coaching business, in which she specialises in working with business people and medical professionals. She positions her service in the following manner. 'I am a leading coach who can work with you, whatever your challenge. I have 15 years of experience in coaching after achieving a Diploma in coaching from XYZ Institute. I am also a qualified Hypnotherapist, an NLP Practitioner and EFT Practitioner, and I'm also a qualified psychiatrist. I use a range of coaching tools to help you reach your goals and overcome your challenges a lot quicker than you would be able to ordinarily. I take a very practical approach to coaching and use tools based on neuroscience and psychology. My clients have included leading businesses and medical professionals.

My fees are as follows –

- Single session - £500

- Block of 4 sessions - £1600
- Block of 8 sessions - £3500

Whilst the above isn't necessarily a bad way to position her service, it's not the optimal way. The above focuses a lot on her coaching. It focuses on her qualifications, experience and method of coaching but it doesn't explain any of the benefits it will provide the clients who work with her. It is far more likely that she will suffer from price objections as well because her prospective clients will think she is expensive. They won't be able to justify her high prices in their minds as they won't really understand how she can help them

Below I have repositioned her statement. It is a more effective statement that is likely to win her more business:

I am a leading coach who can work with you whatever the challenge. I have 15 years of experience in life coaching, during which time I have worked with leading business and medical professionals. I have helped them reach their burning goals and solve their pressing challenges through my unique coaching solution. I use a mix of NLP, EFT and hypnotherapy to help my clients rewire their subconscious minds and as a result extinguish their limiting beliefs. By working with me, my clients reduce their fears, increase their confidence, become more self-aware, develop their focus and become more relaxed and stress-free. The coaching tools that I use are very practical and, as a result, initiate deep and effective changes in my clients. If you are looking for a coach who will get you the results that you are looking for, then look no further.

My fees are as follows -

- Single session - £500 – For those who want to experience surface-level changes
- Block of 4 sessions - £1600 – For those who want to experience significant changes and better results
- Block of 8 sessions - £3500 – For those who want to experience deep changes and significant results

In statement 2, Sarah mentions her experience, coaching tools and whom she works with. She does it in a way that demonstrates how it will help her clients. It is far more focused on the results and benefits. Even when it relates to her fees, she explains how each package will help her client. In the first statement, she just listed the prices without an explanation. In statement 2, she provides an explanation as to what each package does for her clients. Positioning is critical when it comes to sales, as it makes a difference to how your customer thinks about your product or service.

This leads me nicely to another aspect of positioning. I've touched on it in the previous point.

In sales, we call it Features, Advantages and Benefits. This is a key aspect when it comes to how you position your products or services. Let me explain:

A feature is the characteristics of your product or service. An advantage is how your product or service helps your customer and the benefit refers to the gains your customer has from using it. So, let's take the following simple example:

Let's say that XYZ ltd sells car alarms. The feature of their alarm might be that it is the fastest tripping alarm in the world - an intruder only has to touch your car, and it is triggered. The advantage is that it serves as a significant deterrent for thieves and prevents car break-ins. The benefit for the client is that it saves them time and money (as it would affect their insurance premiums and the time and inconvenience of going through an insurance claim). It's a simple example but hopefully will illustrate the point. What I have found is that when selling, most people will lead and focus too much on the features. They will tell a customer all of the great characteristics of a product or service without really explaining how it can ultimately benefit them. Some people have said to me that the customer will be able to work out the benefit themselves. They say that sometimes the benefit is obvious, so why point it out? But my response to this is 'Never assume in sales'! You may think that a customer has fully made a link between the feature and the benefit, but they may not have, so always take the time to explain the benefits.

In addition, people sometimes mistake an advantage for a benefit. Let's take the following example:

Joe Bloggs sells online personal training. Part of his statement might say the following: 'By joining my online personal training sessions you will have the benefit of working out from the comfort of your own home. You can have dinner cooking in the background whilst you work out. By working out from home, you are likely not to skip a workout.'

Many people will consider this as the end benefit when it isn't. The following statement includes the benefit:

'By joining my online personal training sessions, you will have the benefit of working out from your own home. You can have dinner cooking in the background whilst you work out. By working out from home, you are likely not to skip a workout. Ultimately this means that you will be saving yourself time and money.'

Critically, the part about saving time and money described the benefit rather than the part about working out from home and being able to put on something to cook in the background. Many people get this wrong.

Some people are very good at selling the benefits and focus on them when selling. However, there is a danger in doing this too much. Furthermore, if the features and advantages aren't explained properly,

115

then the benefits can come across as fake. Let's take the following example to explain this:

Joe Bloggs sells sales training. He says the following to his customers:

'My world-class sales training programme is going to help your business to increase sales, increase profitability, increase market share and help you reach your target as the number one company in your industry.'

Though the above benefits might be true, without some kind of explanation of the features and advantages, they sound far-fetched to the customer. Now, let's take a revised statement:

'My world-class sales training programme has been carefully designed to get the best out of your sales teams. It combines 15 years of my own sales experience, cutting-edge neuroscience, the latest in mind-set and Neuro-Linguistic Programming techniques and the leading sales methods (features). This combination creates a programme that develops your sales team's mindset and sales skill set. Your team will become more driven, more motivated, less fearful, have fewer limiting beliefs, handle clients' objections better and close more business (advantages). As a result, you are more likely to increase sales, increase profitability, increase market share and reach your target as the number one company in your industry (benefits).

In the second statement, Joe Bloggs gave a breakdown (through the features and advantages) of how the benefits could be attained.

In summary, it's important to include all three components when positioning your product or service to your customers.

In sales, it's crucial that you position your products or services effectively. Furthermore, adding a story to your sales pitch can make it come alive and create a more emotional reaction in the people you're selling to.

Chapter 13

One size doesn't fit all

A huge factor when it comes to success in sales is how well you communicate with different kinds of buyers. Not everyone is the same. Not everyone is motivated by the same things. Although it's difficult to read someone's mind, you can at least try to understand what type of person they are and what makes them tick. Traditionally, buyers have been categorised by:

- Age
- Location
- Social status
- Profession

However, modern science and psychology has allowed buyers to be categorised by their personality types as opposed to demographics only.

There are a few components to this. The first thing we will look at is based on the four types of people that comprise DISC personality assessments. DISC assessment tools are behavioural assessment tools, based on the work of Psychologist William Moulton

Marston. In summary, DISC breaks down people into four types:

- Dominant
- Influencer
- Steady
- Consciousness

I'll briefly explain each one and relate them to how they prefer being sold to:

Dominant – These people tend to be direct, dominant, results-orientated, competitive and action-orientated. They tend to dislike small talk, diplomacy and things that take too long. They also tend to be fast-paced, outspoken, questioning and sceptical of others. They tend to know what they want and make their purchasing decisions quickly. The good thing about selling to these types is that you tend to know where you stand with them. They won't waste your time due to the fact that they are quick decision-makers and because they are direct. People who are Dominant tend (although this isn't always the case) to be in senior decision-making roles; therefore, they have the power to make purchasing decisions. The downside to selling to these types is that they won't give you many chances to make an impression and can be turned off from your product or service very quickly. Furthermore, they don't mind a confrontation, and sometimes the sales conversation can feel quite tough. These people will test you, and passing their tests is a requirement for them to feel comfortable buying from you.

Influencers – These people tend to be fast-paced and outspoken. They are also accepting and warm to others. They tend to be extroverted, optimistic and energetic. These people do like small talk, and they prefer to build a relationship with salespeople before making a purchasing decision. The good thing about selling to these types is that they are optimistic and tend to see the good in people and situations. People who have this personality tend to be (although not always the case) salespeople themselves. They like to build connections and like to be sold to. The downside of selling to these people is that they might end up expecting too much from you or your product and therefore you have to manage their expectations.

Steady – These people tend to be accepting and warm as well as cautious and reflective. They tend to be accommodating, humble and softly spoken. These people are friendly; however, they are cautious and as a result are reluctant decision-makers. They like to build a relationship with a salesperson and tend to be quite agreeable. However, they want to be sure before making a decision and, in addition, they tend to be resistant to change. The advantage of selling to these people is that they will make life easy for you. They will be polite and make you feel comfortable when selling. The disadvantage is that they can sometimes end up wasting your time due to their indirectness and avoidance of making a decision.

Conscientious – These people tend to be questioning and sceptical as well as cautious and reflective. In general, they tend to be reserved, systematic and highly detail-oriented people. Typically, these people tend to be in technical roles such as engineers, data scientists, computer programmers etc. They tend to show very little enthusiasm when you sell to them and typically like to consider all their options carefully. The advantage of selling to these people is that if you know your facts and details well and stick to them, they will be won over. Furthermore, once you win their trust, they are less likely to change their mind. The disadvantage of selling to these types is that they are overly reliant on facts and details. They sometimes fail to see the big picture and even though that is often needed, if you focus on the big picture with them, then you will lose them. They also don't like salespeople who are initially overly friendly and salespeople who get too personal, too quickly. They open up slowly and like to focus more on facts than relationships.

Of course, people are usually a combination of all four personality types and it would be a mistake to assume that anyone will present as a stereotype of any of the above. However, most of the time, they are predominantly one of them.

In addition to DISC personality types, there are other ways of categorising buyers based on personality. Some of these are based on NLP Meta Programs. Meta programs are perceptual filters that generally operate out of our conscious awareness. They filter our perception and determine our preferences in how we feel, think and act. Here are three common ones that I've included because I feel they are valuable to know from a sales perspective:

Towards and away from Meta programme

Those who have a Towards Programme are focused on moving towards pleasure. They frequently set and create new goals for themselves. They are goal focused and like hearing about opportunities. Those with an Away From Programme, tend to avoid risk, they are more cautious and they are focused on moving away from or avoiding pain.

So how does knowing this help us when selling? If you are selling to someone who has a Towards Meta Program, then you are better off focusing on what it will mean to them if the goals they have set are achieved. If you are selling to someone who has an Away From Programme, then you are better off focusing on the cost to them of not solving their problem. The following example helps clarify this:

Let's say Joe Bloggs was selling his sales training service to a sales director, who had a Toward Meta Program. He would be better off explaining how his service would help the client's company achieve their sales targets, how it would help him achieve his bonus and help him get a promotion. However, let's say Joe Bloggs was selling his service to a Sales Director who had an away from Meta programme. He would be better off explaining how, if the salespeople in the company did not improve their sales skills, they would lose sales, lose out to the competition, lose market share and even lose their jobs.

Being able to understand which Meta program your customer is more inclined to can help you understand where you should focus your conversation.

Detail and Global Meta Program

Those with a Detail Meta Program are more concerned with the specifics of a situation. They like to know the details. Those with a Global Meta Program prefer to look at things from the big picture, speak in general terms and avoid specifics. Let's use the same example of Joe Bloggs selling his sales training service to a sales director of a company. If Joe Bloggs was selling to someone with a Global Meta program, then he would talk about how sales training would help the sales reps gain more confidence, more clarity and more self-belief. Furthermore, how the training would help the company grow their sales, its market share and ultimately, its brand. If he was selling to a person who had a Detailed Meta Program, then he would talk about what his training programme included, how many hours of training they would receive and the nature of his training methodology.

Sameness and Difference Meta Program-

Those with a Sameness Meta Program generate understanding by looking for similarities with previous experience. Repetition doesn't bore them. They prefer something tried and tested as it instils comfort. Those with a Difference Meta Program don't mind the unknown. They prefer variety and change. So, let's apply this to an example of Joe Bloggs selling. If he was selling his training services to a Sales Director who had a Sameness Meta Program, then he would talk about the ease of implementing his training. If the company already used sales training, then he would talk about how this would make it easier for them to implement his programme, as they already have it in place. If he was talking to a Sales Director who had a Difference Meta Program, he would talk about how his training provides something they have never had before. How his training would provide something new and that in order to get better results they would need to try a fresh approach.

To identify someone's DISC personality or Meta Programme filter can be a really powerful tool when selling. You're able to adjust your sales pitch and style to the person that you are selling to. I have found that too many people have a one size fits all when it comes to sales and sell to their customers in the same style. They are then puzzled why the relationship broke down or why their customers didn't buy from them. The way you obtain an understanding of your customer's Meta program and DISC style, comes down to the questions you ask them and really listening to the language they use in their response. Simply being aware of the above can really help.

Chapter 14

Influence me.

A critical element of success in sales is how well we can influence other people. Notice I use the word influence and not manipulate. Many people get this word (or the meaning of this word) confused when it comes to sales. For me, influencing is when you attempt to persuade your customer to see the benefits of using your product or service. The key thing is that they must have a genuine need for your product or service, and you must be able to serve that need. If it doesn't meet those two criteria, then it's considered to be manipulation if you continue to sell to them. If it does meet those criteria, then you must do all you can to influence them.

There have been numerous books written about influencing. They have ranged from influencing when selling to influencing at a more general level. In life, we are always trying to influence. A parent might try to influence their child into eating more healthy food. An environmental activist might try to influence a group of people to use more sustainable resources. A psychiatrist might try influencing their patient who suffers from low self-esteem, to believe that they are a valuable person. The list goes on. Let's look at influence when it comes to sales.

I believe that people will ultimately buy from people that they know, like and trust. If you can establish all three with a customer then you are far more likely to influence their buying decision. Let's break down all three in a little more detail when it comes to sales.

Know – This is all about exposure. How often is your customer exposed to you? In the modern day, this includes online as well as offline exposure. You want to get your prospective customer to know you as much as possible, even before you directly sell to them. This can include posting through social media and hosting webinars, podcasts and infomercials. It also includes sending them valuable content and information and regularly attending networking events. Basically, it means doing anything that exposes you to them so that when you sell directly to them, they feel they already know you. It's a very important part of the sales process as it means that, psychologically, buyers feel safe when you are selling to them.

Like – Humans are ultimately emotional creatures. There is a famous saying which says, 'We tend to buy with emotion and justify with logic.' Often, we will buy from someone if we like them. Furthermore, as humans, the majority of us have an intrinsic need to be liked. As I explained earlier in the book, this is due to evolution. When we were living in tribes, if we did something that others deemed wrong and which caused them to dislike us, we would be removed from the tribe. As a result, we would have most probably faced death, as we couldn't survive the harsh terrains by ourselves. So, this need to be liked and to like other people has been built into our core.

So how and why do people end up liking us? First, it's important to reiterate that different people will like different types of people, so this isn't a one size fits all. However, there are some common themes that arise with most people.

People who are similar to us – We tend to like people who act, think and even look similar to us. That's why body language techniques, such as mirroring, can be so effective. Mirroring is when you subtly copy or mirror the body language of the other person. Let's consider the different buyer types we spoke about in the last chapter. Buyers will be more inclined to like sellers who match their personality or Meta programme type. I am a big believer in being yourself when selling (or anything in life, for that matter). Don't try to change yourself or deviate massively from your natural style just to please someone else when selling. However, we can certainly appeal to their similarities and tweak our communication style and what we talk about so that they feel we are similar. By doing this and at the same time not sacrificing our core self, we are more likely to persuade them to like us.

Talking about them and their interests – People love to talk about themselves. They like it when their needs, wants and desires are focused upon. They like it when people have taken out the time and effort to understand them. I am still surprised at the extent to which salespeople will talk about themselves and their product or service when having conversations with clients. A golden rule when selling is to speak less than the client. Use the principle of we have two ears and one mouth and communicate in that proportion. A client is not likely to warm to us if we talk to them, tell them everything about us, our product, our company etc, and ask nothing about them. They need a chance to talk. So, when you communicate with a customer (especially the first couple of times), it's better to be more interested in what they have to say than what you have to say. It's better to ask those questions and talk about their interests and what they want. If you do this, they are much more inclined to like you.

Give appreciation and avoid criticism – Whilst this is more of an issue for people who are managing a team, it is also relevant when speaking with customers. Whilst it's very unlikely that a salesperson will criticise a customer to their face, they are also just as unlikely to give appreciation. People love to be acknowledged and appreciated and they will usually love the person who gives them this positive response. I would like to stress that it must be sincere appreciation and not what they deem as lip service.

So, if you like something about your customer, their working style, their product, service or their company, then vocalise it. Let them (and others) know what you think. You will be surprised by the benefits that you receive by doing this.

Use their name – It is often said that the favourite word a person can hear is the sound of their name. When you speak with anyone, remember to use their name. I always remember a particular networking event that I attended many years ago. I was speaking with four of my colleagues at the time, and a gentleman approached our group. Introductions were made, and then, over the next few minutes, while he spoke with us, he addressed each of us by our names. I remember taking a step back and looking at how engaged my colleagues were with him. In fact, every time he mentioned their name, their ears would prick up, and they would give him their full attention. I remember being very impressed with this man, not only because he had managed to remember everyone's name so quickly but how he was weaving it into his conversation. When you use people's names, they like it, and they tend to start liking you.

Trust

For me, trust is the most important aspect when it comes to influencing someone. People might know and like you but if they don't trust you then they will never buy from you. Trust comes in many forms. Let's explore them below:

Sincerity – People must believe that you are being genuine and sincere in what you say. They can't think that you are saying whatever it takes to make the sale happen. Unfortunately, this is the presumption that most customers have when they are speaking to salespeople. That is why being honest can be such a powerful tool to gain people's trust. Yes, you might have to be somewhat diplomatic when being honest (you don't want to offend people), but you should always aim to be as open as possible. One of the best ways to do this when selling is, to be honest about your weaknesses or any limitations of your product or service. Many salespeople will try to avoid this or sugar-coat the weaker aspects of their product. However, customers often see through this, and it breaks their trust. When a customer sees that you are open and honest about what you can't deliver, they will automatically trust you more. Always go into a sale trying to do what's right by the customer. If you have this mentality then your actions will match and you will gain the customer's trust.

Confidence – In order for someone to trust in what you say, they must also have confidence in you. They must feel confident that you will deliver on your promises and that you are equipped to help them. That is why in modern selling it's so important to come across as an authority in your industry, product or service. If, for example, you were selling IT software, then it would be important that you knew a lot about the IT industry, the needs of customers in the industry and your product or service. Modern buyers are looking for vendors that can provide them with advice and alternative, unique solutions to their problems. It is therefore very important that you can demonstrate knowledge and credibility so that your customers will trust you.

Knowledge and appearing to be an authority are great, however, it's also very important that you sound and look confident when speaking to a customer. I am surprised that some people will mumble their words, speak in a low, monotone voice or avoid eye contact when selling. Buyers want to feel, see and hear your confidence. When you communicate with confidence they will trust you.

Social /external validation/ proof- The most powerful way for people to believe what you say is when other people confirm it. When somebody else sings your praises then it is much more believable than when you sing your own. That is why client testimonials, for example, are so powerful. So in order to get prospective customers to trust you, find ways to encourage them to see your testimonials and case studies. Persuade them to speak with your existing clients if possible.

When customers know, trust and like you then the chance of influencing them is much higher. There is one other topic to consider in relation to influencing.

Empowering your customer – One of the main reasons people don't buy is often because they do not trust themselves to make the right decision. In fact it is often the case that buyers end up making no decision at all, and fail to buy from anyone, even a competitor. In many cases, they would rather make no decision than a decision that could be wrong. That is why it is so important for you to empower your prospective customer so that they feel confident in themselves to make a purchasing decision.

I will repeat the story from earlier in the book of the client who came to me and said that he wanted to have more gravitas in front of his clients. He didn't think that they took him seriously enough and he didn't command enough authority. He said he wanted to know how he could impress them more. I immediately changed his focus from trying to impress them, to trying to empower them. You will gain far more influence with someone when you empower them, than when you are merely trying to impress them. Furthermore, they will respect and like you more by doing this. I am sure there have been occasions in your life when someone has tried too hard to impress you. I am sure that not only have you found it highly annoying but you have probably found it to be insincere. So how do you empower your prospective clients?

The best way to do this is to remind them of times when they have made a good purchasing decision. It is a poor strategy to get the client to remember bad experiences they have had with your competitors. Some salespeople think that by doing that it will make the prospective customer look at their product or service more favourably compared to that of their competitors. However, it often has the opposite effect. When people are reminded of bad experiences they have had, it also reminds them of bad decisions they have made and this disempowers them from making a decision in the present moment. It fills their heads with self-doubt and their minds focus on the dangers. It is far better to encourage them to remember positive experiences they have had when they purchased a product or service. Get them to remember the great decisions they have made. By doing this, you are reminding them to trust their decision-making skills which empowers them and makes it more likely that they will make a decision to work with you. Furthermore, when people are in an empowered, positive thinking state they are more likely to be action-oriented and this further increases the likelihood of them making a decision.

Influencing is a huge topic in itself and could be considered in a lot more detail. Maybe I will devote a whole book to the subject in the future. For now, remember that in order to influence anyone they have to know, trust and like you and feel empowered to make a buying decision.

Chapter 15

Always be closing

When I mention the word closing, I find many people screw their faces up. They hate the thought of closing someone else. However, all closing really means is to get someone over the line. It means getting a prospective customer to make that final decision and to sign a cheque. So first of all, just get comfortable with the word!

People often think of great closing as some magic conversation that happens at the end of the sales process. They think of it as some amazing final words that the person selling delivers in order to finally convince the customer. They often even think of it as one final conversation where all the stars align, and the sale is made. The reality is that this couldn't be further from the truth. The truth about closing is that it takes place the moment that you have your first-ever interaction with the customer. Closing actually takes place from the beginning of the sales process and continues all the way to the end. It does not start and finish all in one conversation at the end of the process.

Effectively closing is everything that we have spoken about in this book. Closing begins with having a rock-solid inner game. It's when you reach out to a customer, it's how you approach them, how much you understand their needs, the questions you ask, the way you listen to them, and the way you speak. It's whether they trust, know and like you. It's the whole gambit. It's very important that people realise this for a number of important reasons.

Firstly, it is a mistake to wait for some big conversation at the end of the sales process, where you will be able to bamboozle the client, really impress them and get them over the line. The chances are that this will never happen, as the client may have decided not to buy from you during the sales process. Secondly, it really helps to think with the end in mind. Your end goal is for the customer to buy from you (assuming there is a genuine need, of course). Therefore, you should be doing all you can to make this happen from your very first interaction. I have found the mentality of leaving everything to the end to be a massive detriment to the sale happening.

Closing is an ongoing process and involves multiple touch points. Furthermore, closing doesn't always mean making the sale happen in every conversation. Closing can often mean just closing the next step in a process. It can mean getting a prospect to agree to a demonstration of your product or for them to set up a meeting with their boss, who is the decision maker. Often people will think of closing only as making the final sale and, as a result, forget to close all the mini-steps needed to make the sale. Ultimately the point I am trying to make is that closing is actually about taking the client through a journey throughout the sales process. It's not about some magical conversation at the end. Remember to implement this advice, and you will be much more likely to win the sale.

Final thoughts

When it comes to sales, it's important that you work continuously on getting your mindset right. You need to become super self-aware. You need to explore the relationship that you have with yourself, with sales and with your product or service.

You need to have complete clarity about what you are trying to achieve and why this is important to you. You need to explore your values and align them to your goals in order to be clear on what you want, why you want it and who you need to become to get it.

You need to gain control of your subconscious thoughts and make them work for you. Remove the limiting beliefs, reduce your fears and focus on what you want as opposed to what you're afraid of. You need to work actively on developing your confidence and self-belief so that you genuinely believe in yourself and, as a result, take the necessary action needed to achieve successful outcomes.

You need to create a positive and winning mindset so you are playing to win and not just to compete.

In addition to developing your mindset, you also need to work on developing those key sales skills.

You must learn to ask intelligent and powerful questions so that you understand the client's goals and pain points. You must learn to gather the information that not only allows you to ascertain if you can genuinely help them but also that you can address their needs when talking about your product or service. Questions also help clients understand their own problems, challenges and goals better.

You must work on how you position your products or service so that it appeals to your customer and focuses on not only how you can help them, but also how it will ultimately benefit them.

You must become a powerful listener. The best way to achieve this is to focus on really trying to understand your customers' needs and not simply responding with something to impress them.

Remember that different people are motivated by different things and your job when selling is to try to understand your buyer's personality type and intrinsic motivations. This is so that you can tailor your conversation and focus on what is most likely to appeal to them. You must try to understand their buyer type.

Remember that no one will buy from you unless they know, like and trust you. Therefore, you must do all you can to ensure these three boxes are ticked off in the mind of the customer. This relies on being sincere, demonstrating competence and confidence and engaging with them as much as possible.

Remember that closing a sale is ultimately the most important step when it comes to working with a customer. However, the closing process happens right throughout the sale. You need to continuously demonstrate value to your customer from initial contact right through to the end.

I wrote this book to give an overview of what I believe to be the key factors of success in developing sales from both a mindset and a skillset perspective. It is a distillation of my knowledge and philosophy in these areas. I wanted to make it a quick and easy read and therefore there are opportunities for readers to explore some areas in more detail, but I believe it covers the fundamentals of my philosophy and should provide everyone with a firm basis for moving forward to greater success.

I hope that you have found it an interesting, informative and valuable read. I hope that it can take you, your sales, your business and ultimately your lives to the next level.

I'll end with one of my favourite quotes by Benjamin Franklin:

'For the best return on money, pour your purse into your head.'

The fact that you purchased this book and read it, means that you're embracing the philosophy of Mr Franklin.

Good luck on your journey!

Acknowledgements

I would like to thank many people for being part of my life and for being part of the journey that ultimately allowed me to write this book.

Firstly, I would like to thank my family for being part of my life from day one, for all they have done for me and for providing me with inspiration. I would like to thank all of my close friends (they know who they are), for being part of my life and sharing so many special memories with me. I would like to thank the teachers and gurus that I have used over the years and who have helped me to better understand myself and take myself to the next level in my personal development. I would like to thank the great managers I have had in my career who helped me to develop into a great salesperson. I would like to thank the famous athletes, leaders and business people whom I follow for inspiration and whose behaviour I look to imitate. People such as Michael Jordan, Sachin Tendulkar, Virat Kohli, Mike Tyson, Christiano Ronaldo, Kobe Bryant, Connor Mcgregor, Muhammad Ali, Henry Ford, Steve Jobs, Oprah Winfrey, Tony Robbins, Tim Grover, Dr Jon Demartini and Grant Cardone to name but a few.

I would also like to thank all of my clients who have had faith in me, opened up to me and invested in me. The clients who give me the motivation to keep improving, working on myself and growing my business.

I would also like to thank the Divine Force in the Universe (God, Spirit, Cosmic Energy) for being on my side and giving me those moments of luck when I've needed them.

About the Author

Navin Jaitly is an award-winning salesman, speaker and international best-selling author. After spending 15 years in corporate sales, he trained to become an accredited coach and created his business Navin Jaitly Coaching Ltd. He is on a mission to inspire, empower and develop salespeople, sales leaders and entrepreneurs across the world. Navin transformed himself from a struggling salesperson to an award-winning one, through intense personal development. He worked on developing both his mindset and skillset in order to reach high performance. He now works with sales professionals, leaders, business owners and professional athletes and helps them achieve peak performance.

He is passionate about helping people to transform themselves and reach their full potential.

Book summary

When it comes to sales performance, the focus has traditionally centred on developing a person's sales skill set. Whilst this is very important, what often gets neglected is developing their mindset and helping them achieve emotional mastery. If ultimately, we are the product of our thoughts that lead to our emotions, then it only makes sense that we should prioritise developing them. This book looks at the strategies and tools that anyone involved in sales can use in order to transform themselves from the inside out. It also looks at how they can develop their sales skills in order to further drive-up performance.

If you are a salesperson, sales leader or business owner, then this is an essential read. This will help you transform your performance and results for life. It's a book that combines personal development and sales techniques in order to help you maximise your sales potential.

This isn't just another sales book. It is an alternative look at how to develop sales performance.

Printed in Great Britain
by Amazon